OLAF BREUNING
Drawings

VERLAG FÜR MODERNE KUNST

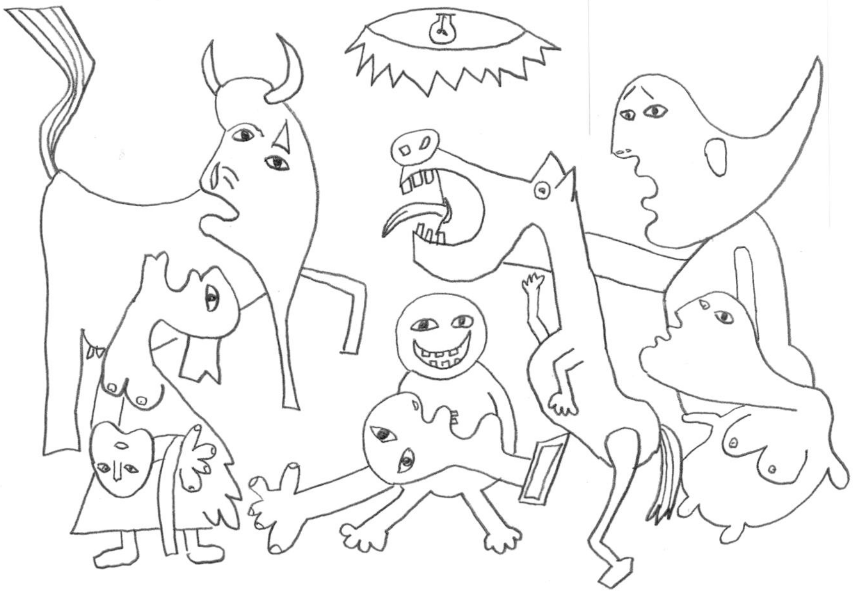

There Is Always Someone Smiling
2010

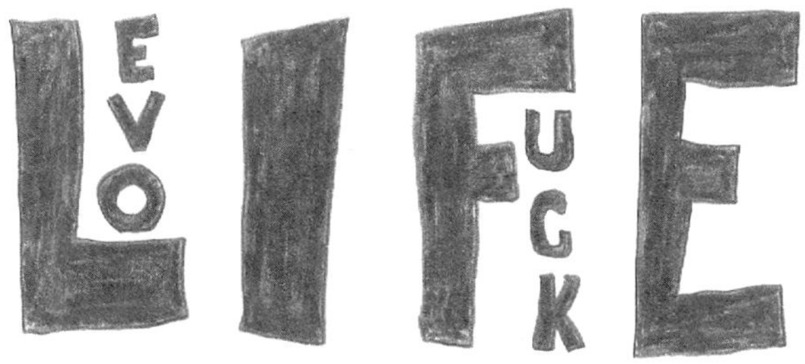

Love Life Fuck
2011

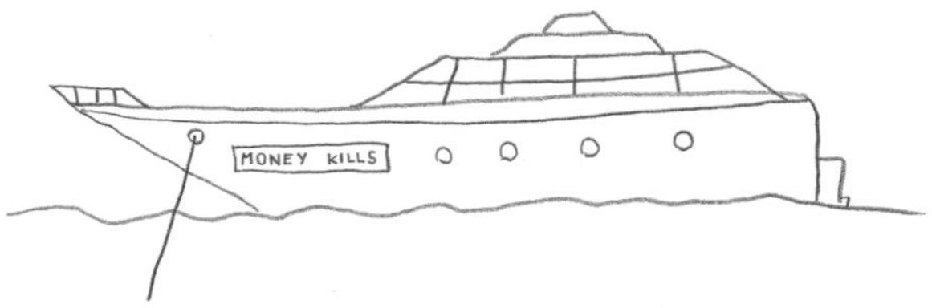

Money Kills
2014

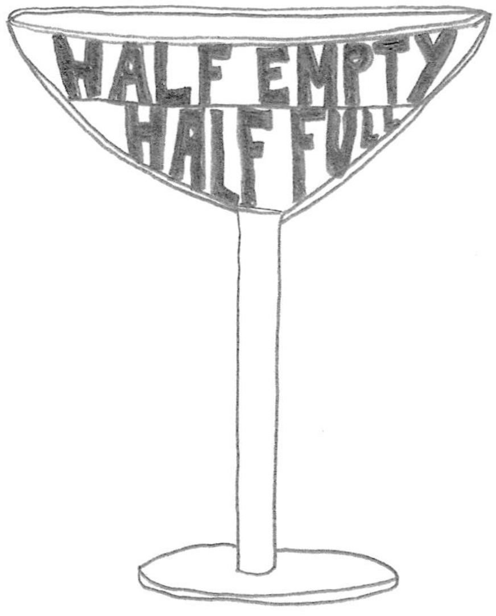

Half Empty Half Full
2009

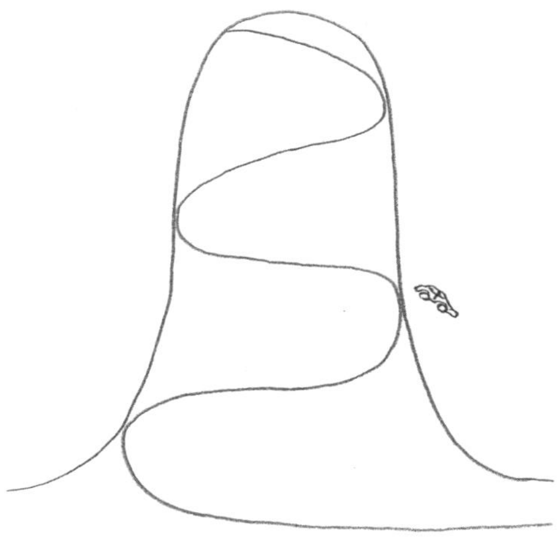

Too Fast
2016

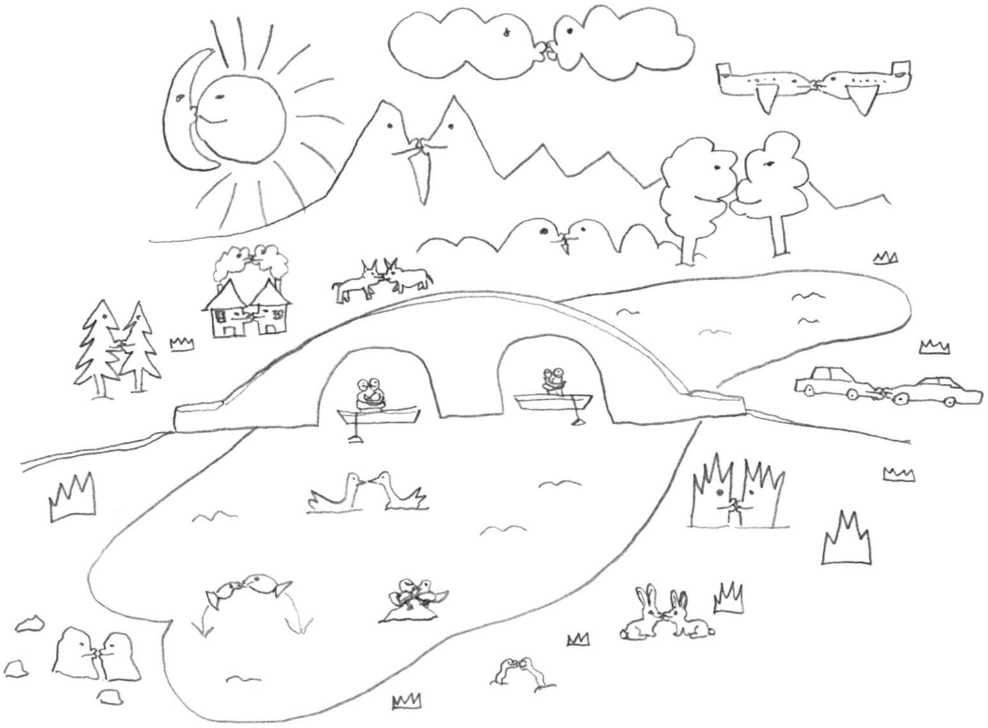

Sound of Love
2007

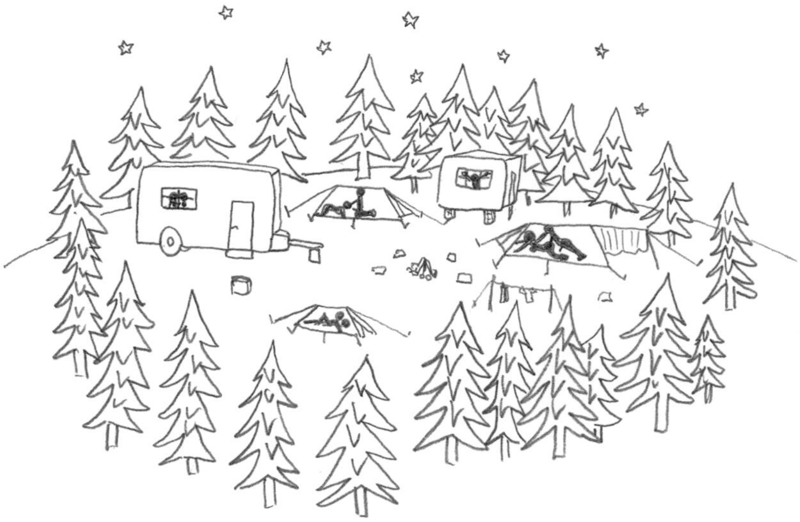

Camping at Night
2009

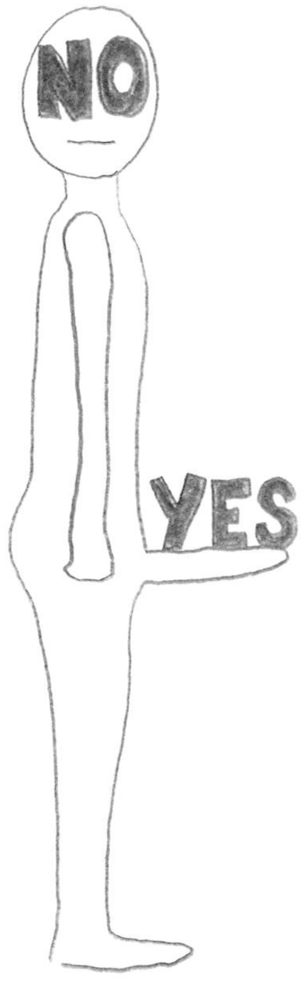

Yes / No
2009

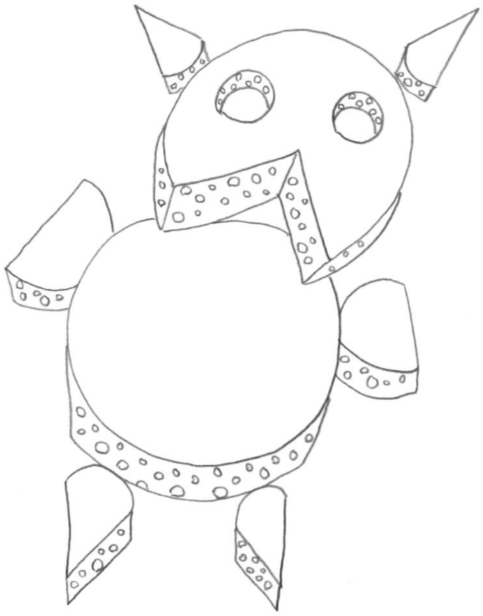

I Am Swiss
2005

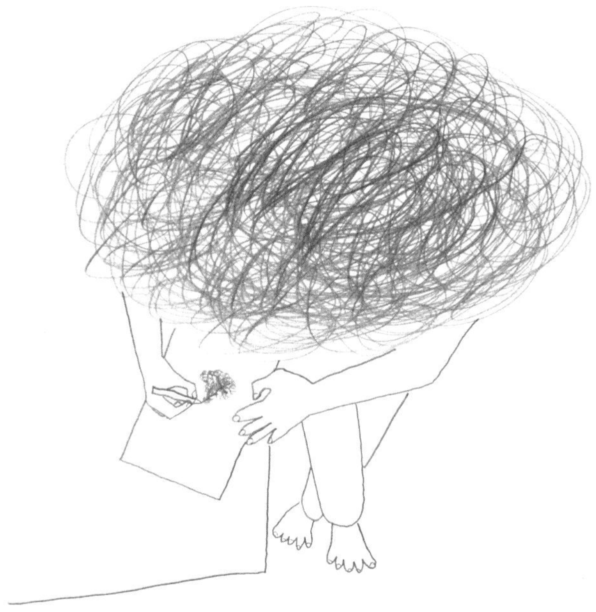

Chaos in There
2010

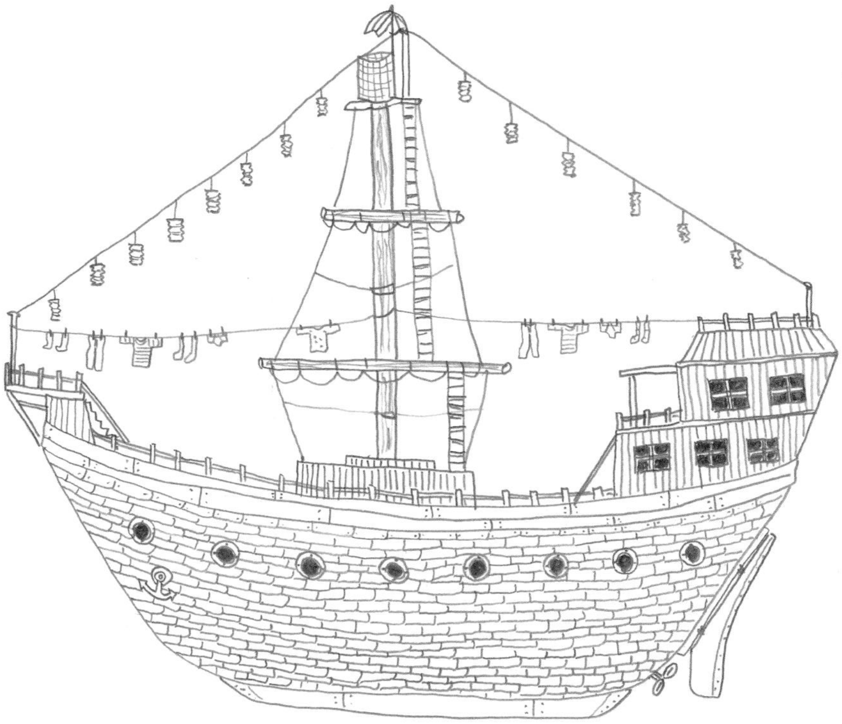

Simple Home
2005

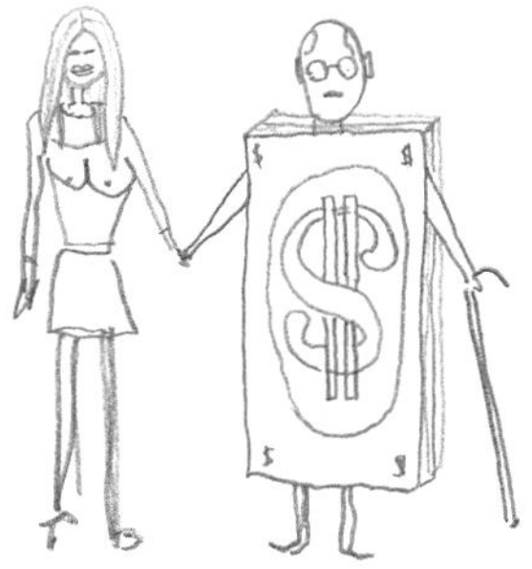

Chicken Head
2008

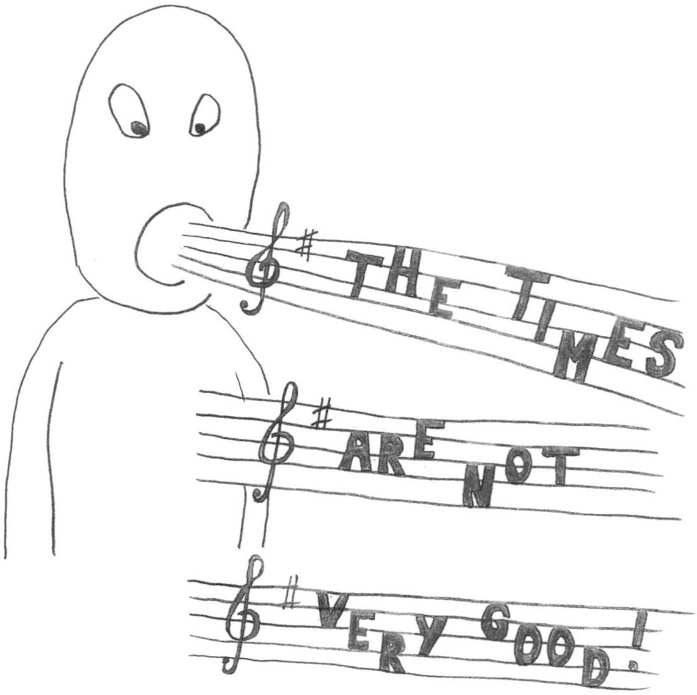

Bad Times
2007

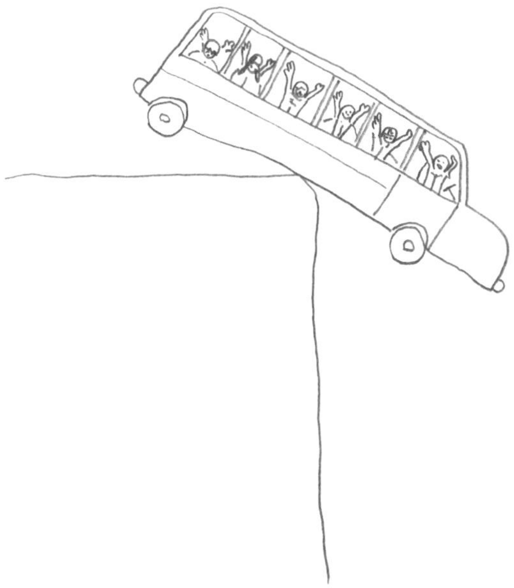

Poor Students
2009

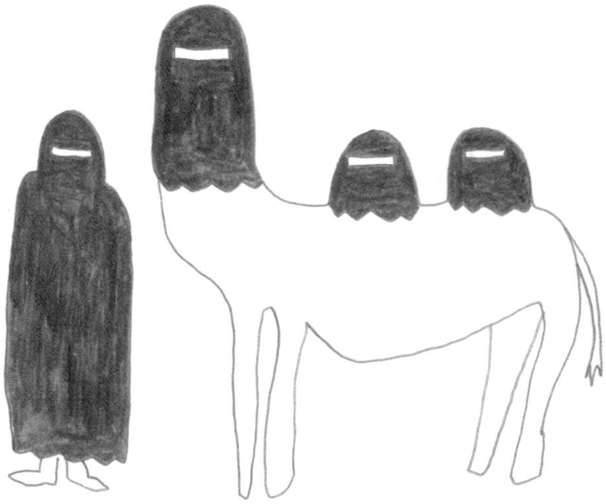

Allah Is Big
2005

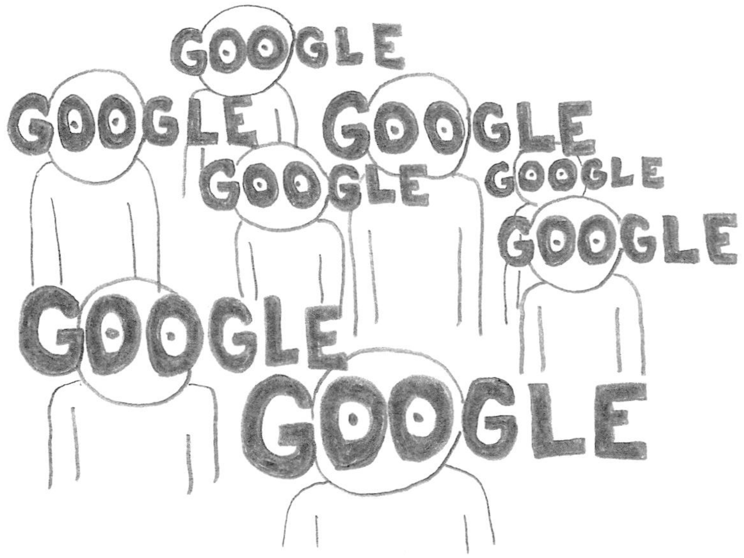

Google
2008

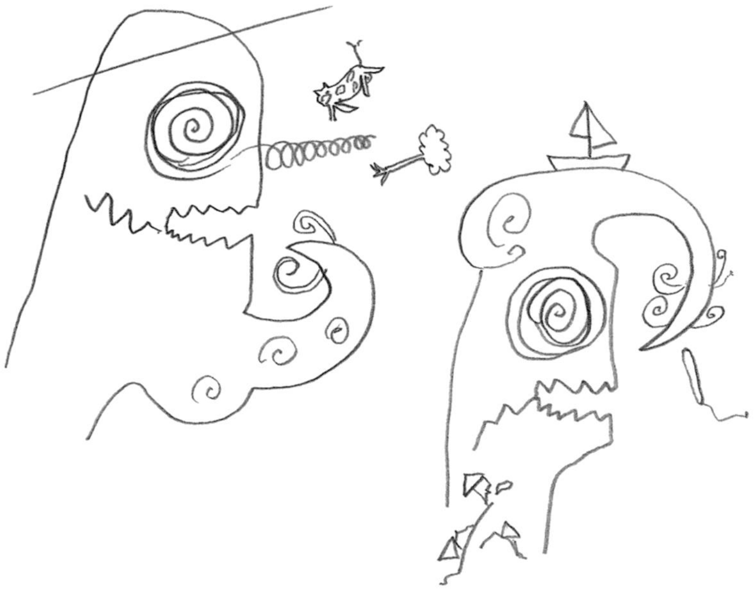

Tsunami, Earthquake and Hurricane
2006

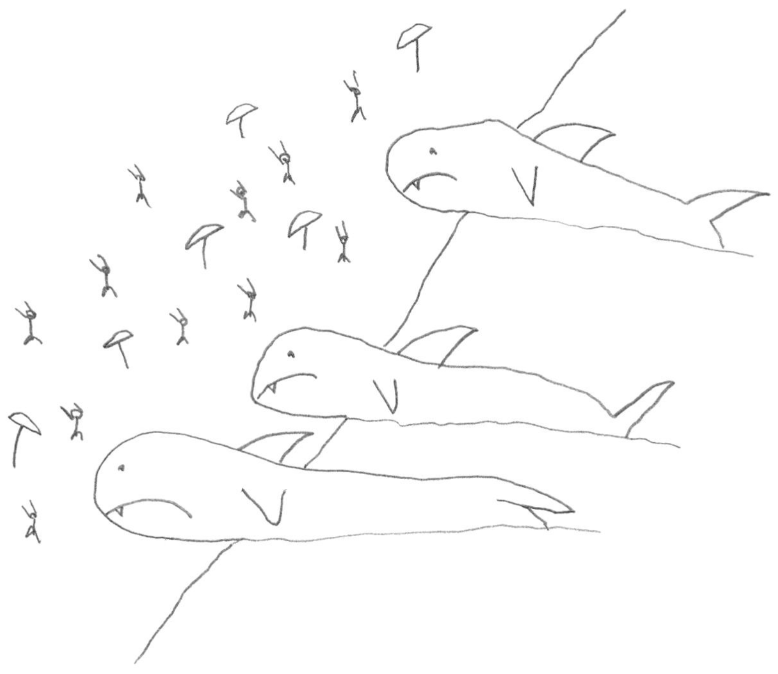

Invasion
2008

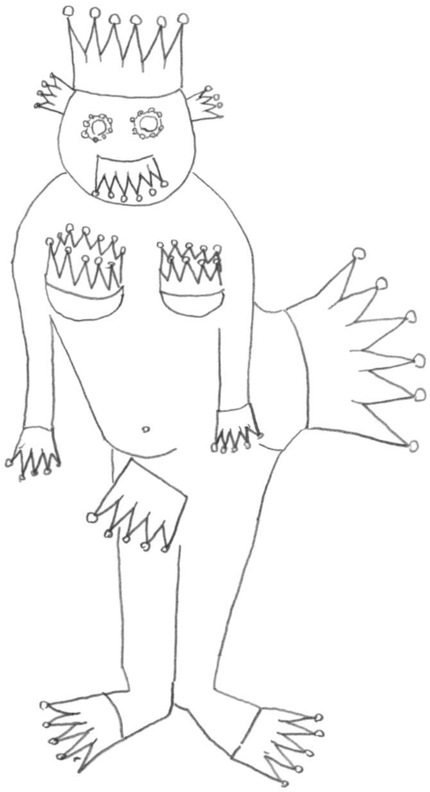

King Again
2006

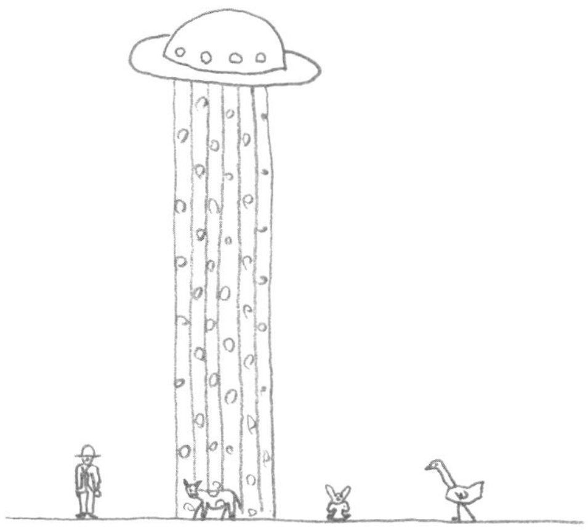

The Selection
2013

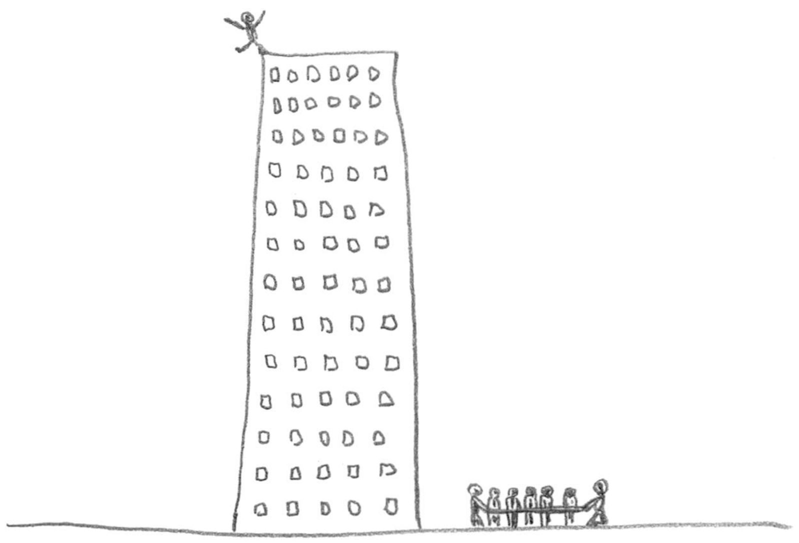

Wrong Side
2008

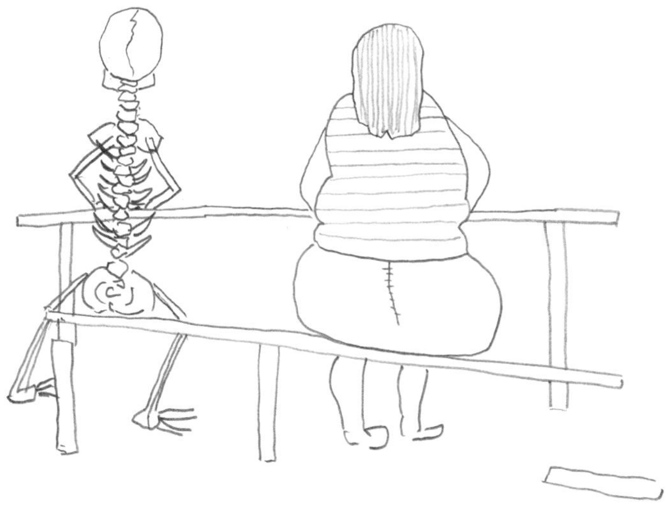

Skinny and Fat
2005

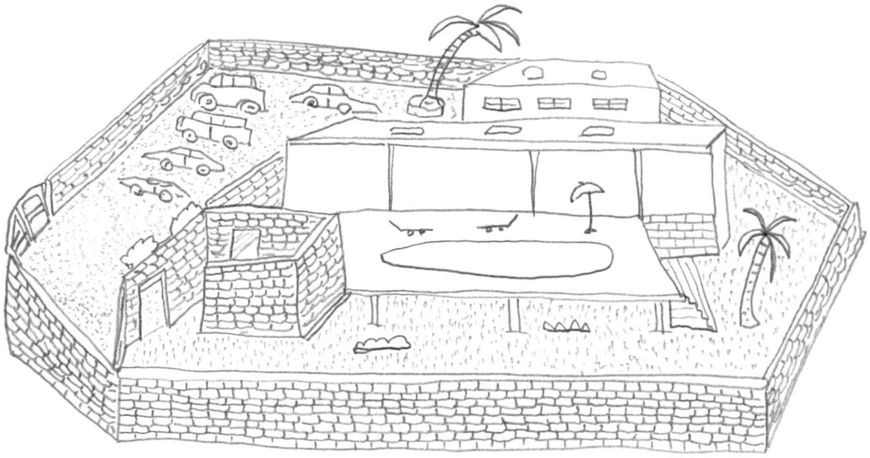

Hollywood Mansion
2007

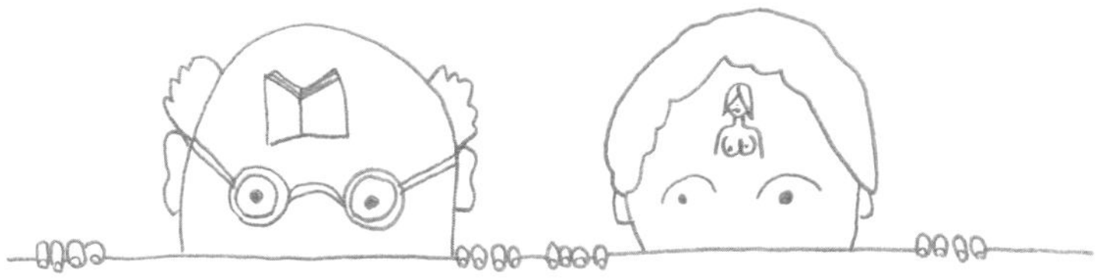

Boobs or Books
2012

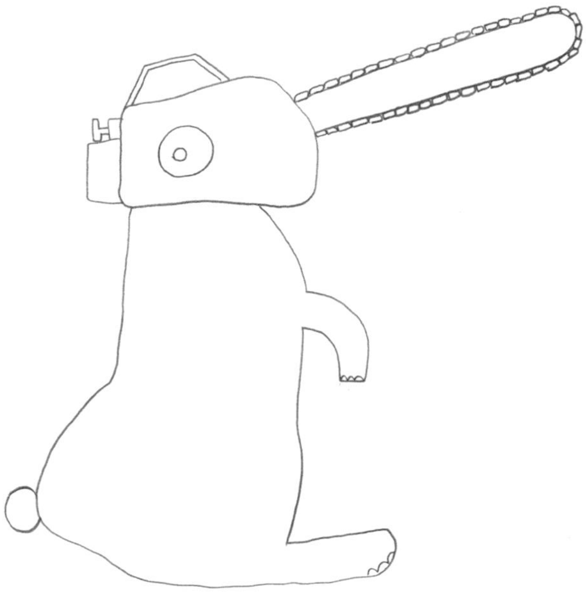

Chainsaw Bear
2005

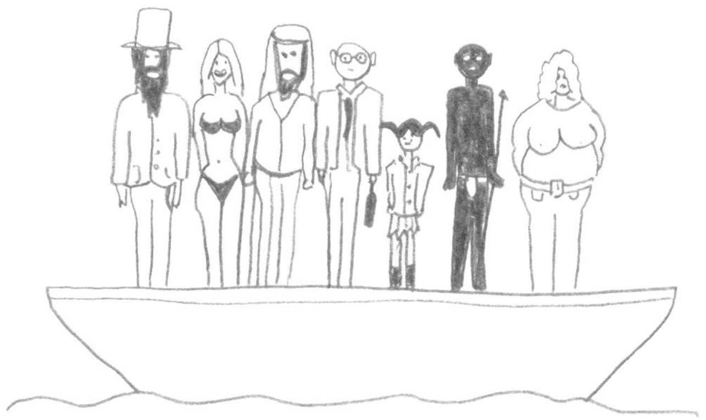

We Are All in the Same Boat
2012

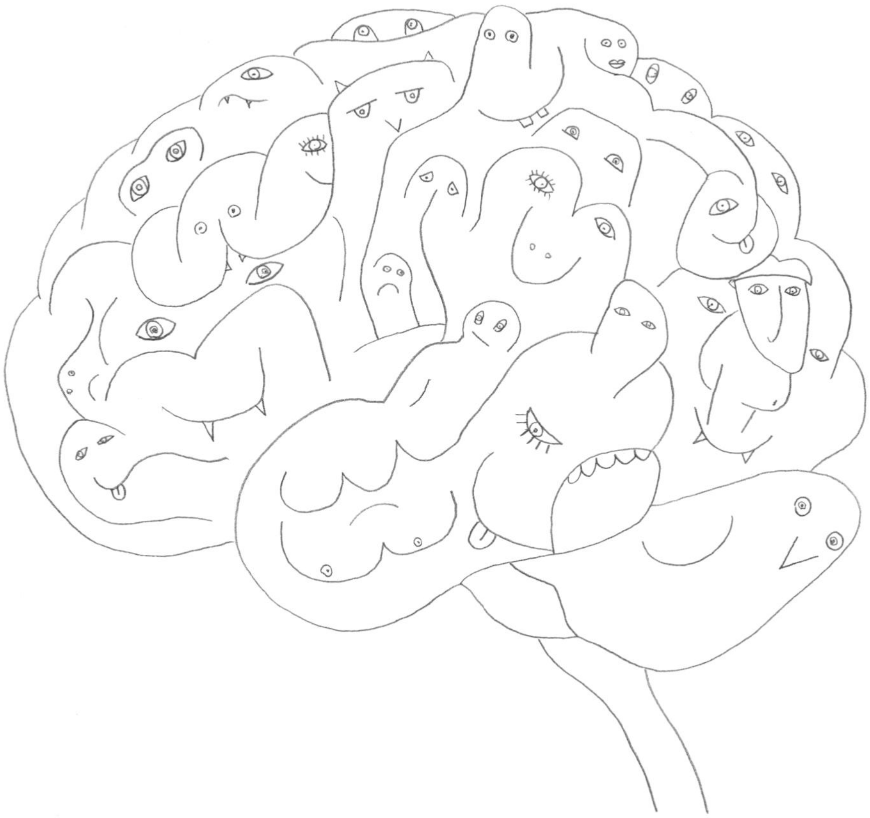

I Don’t Wanna Know What Is in My Brain
2007

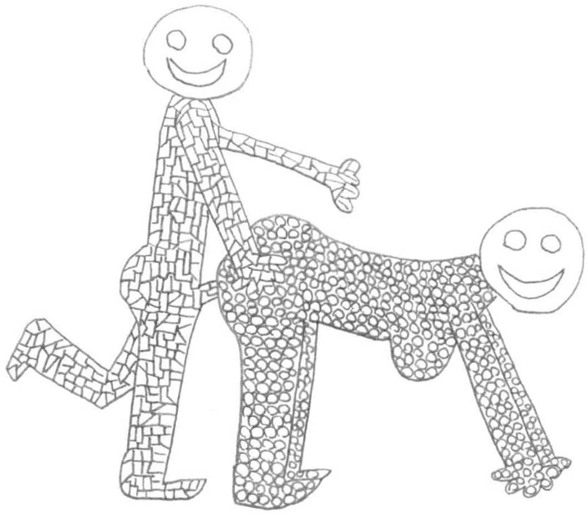

Mosaic Fuck
2007

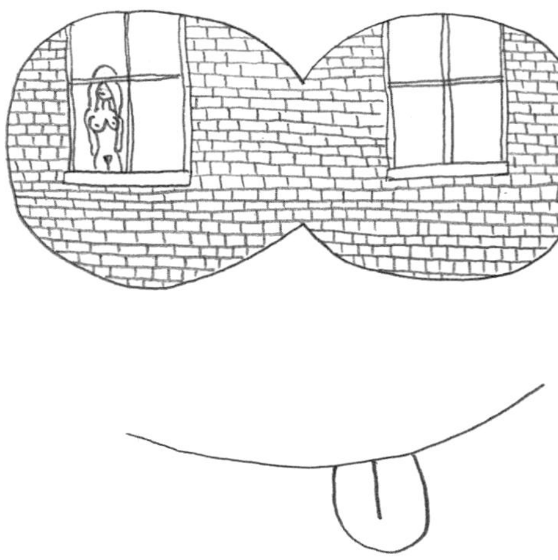

Pervert
2007

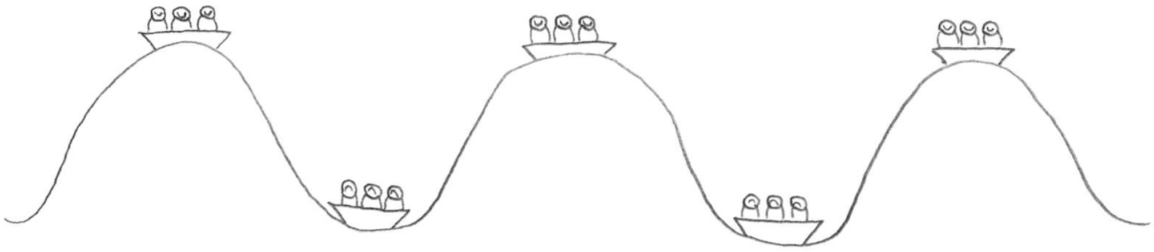

Up and Down
2007

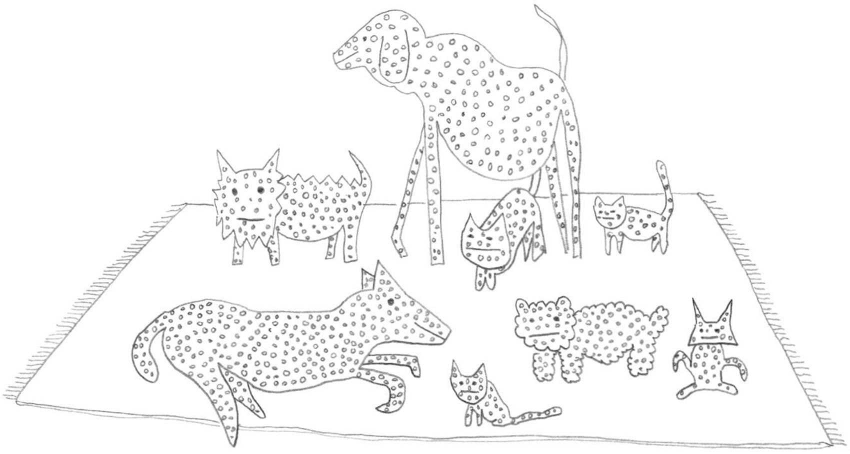

A Lot of Animals Looking Good on a Carpet
2005

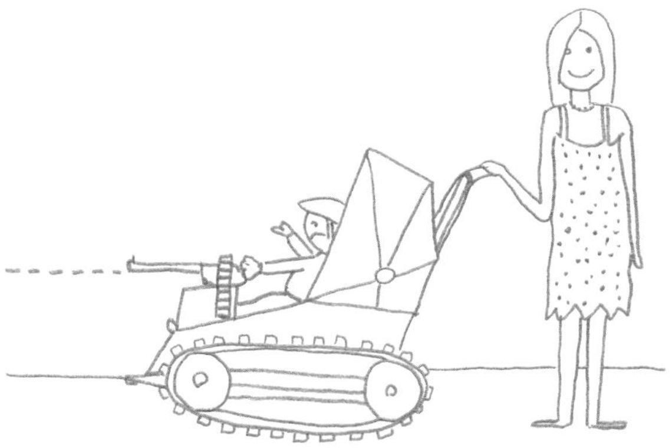

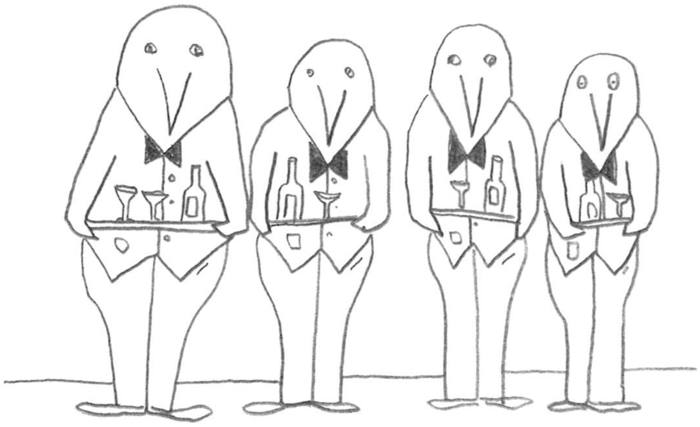

Waiters Should Be Penguins
2007

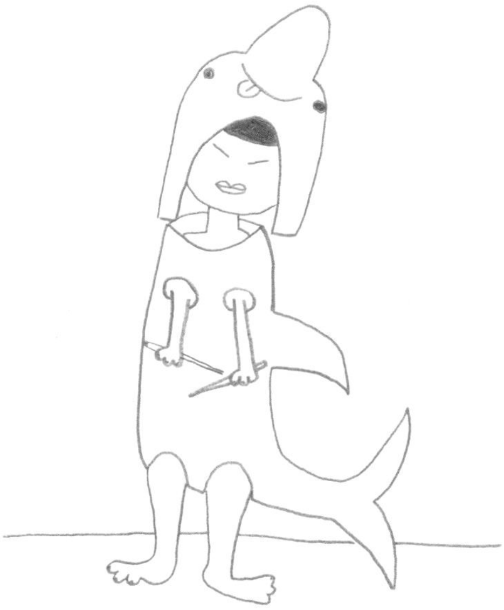

Sushi Girl
2011

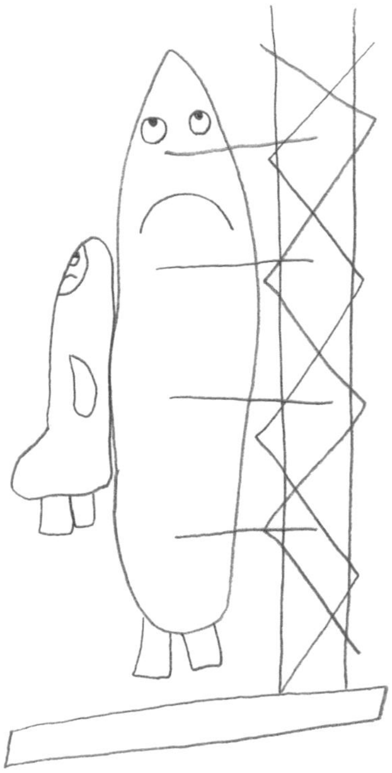

Not so Confident
2014

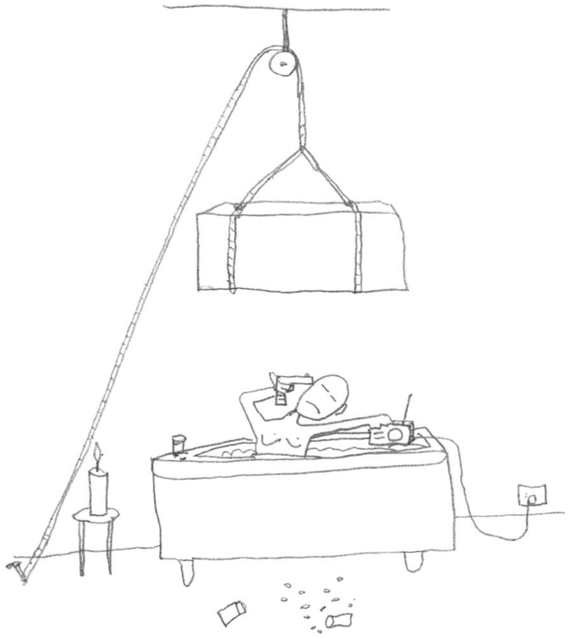

This Time It Will Work
2007

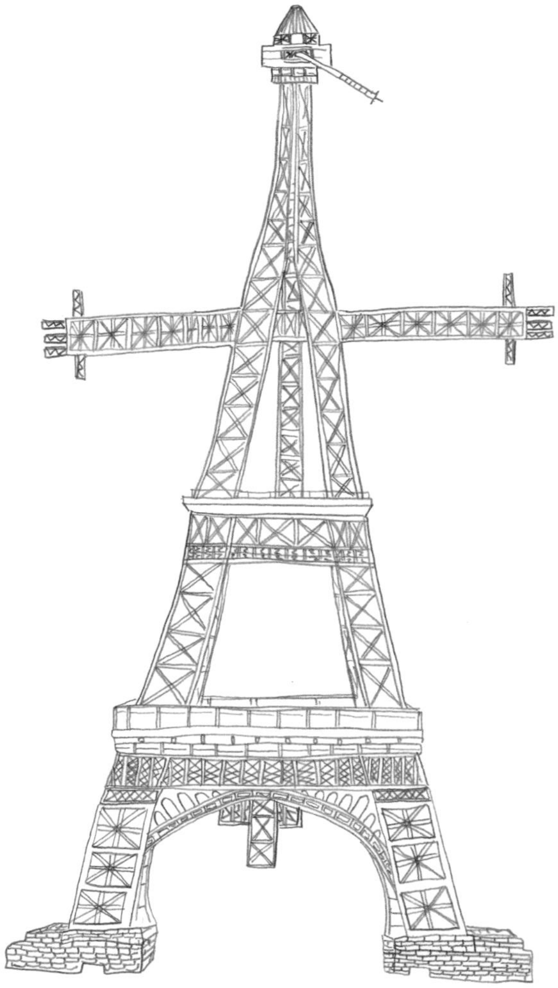

Paris Is Nice
2005

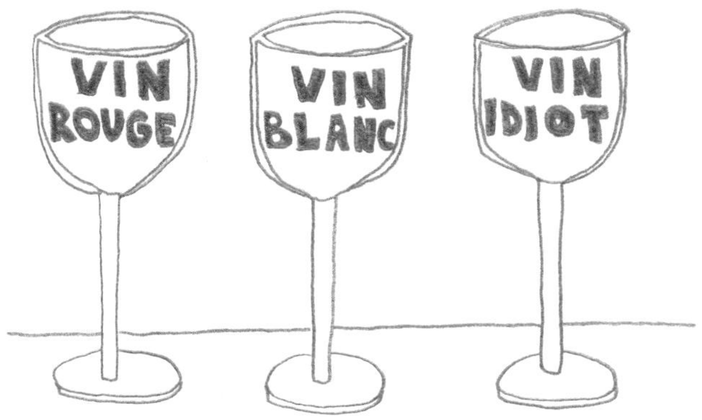

Vin Idiot
2012

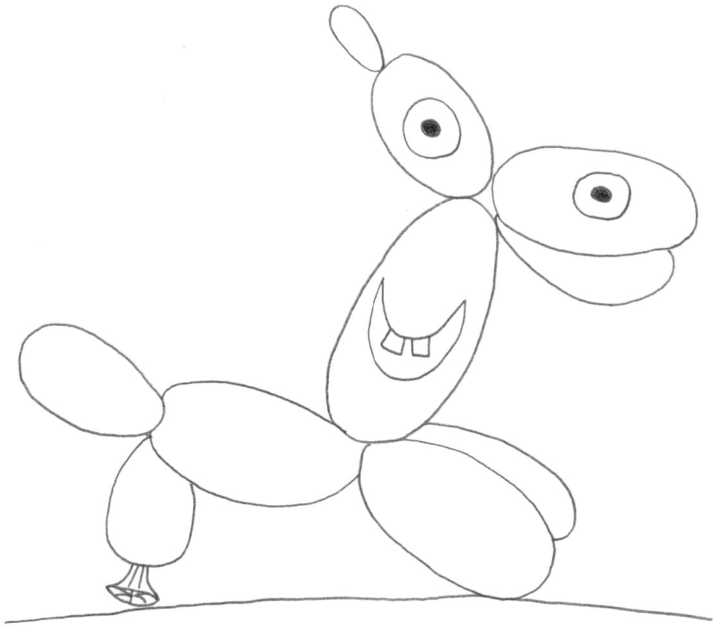

Just Turn It Around Jeff
2005

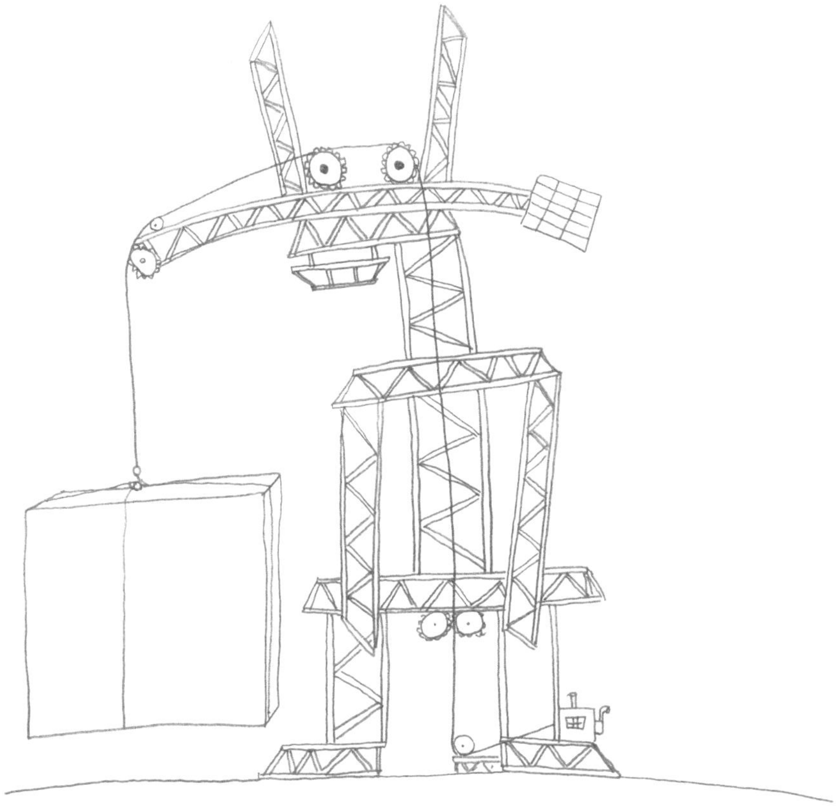

Sad Crane
2013

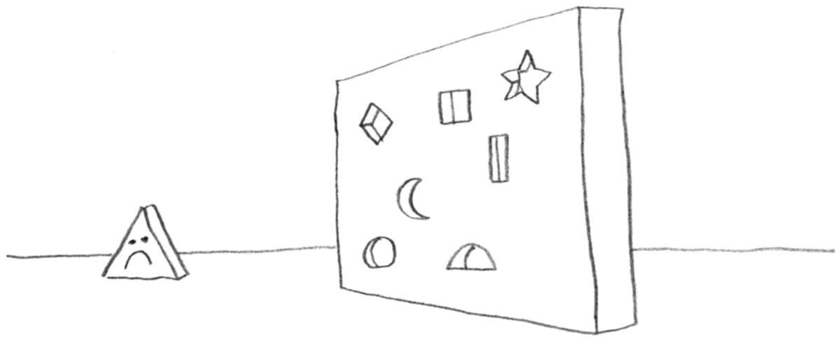

No Shape
2007

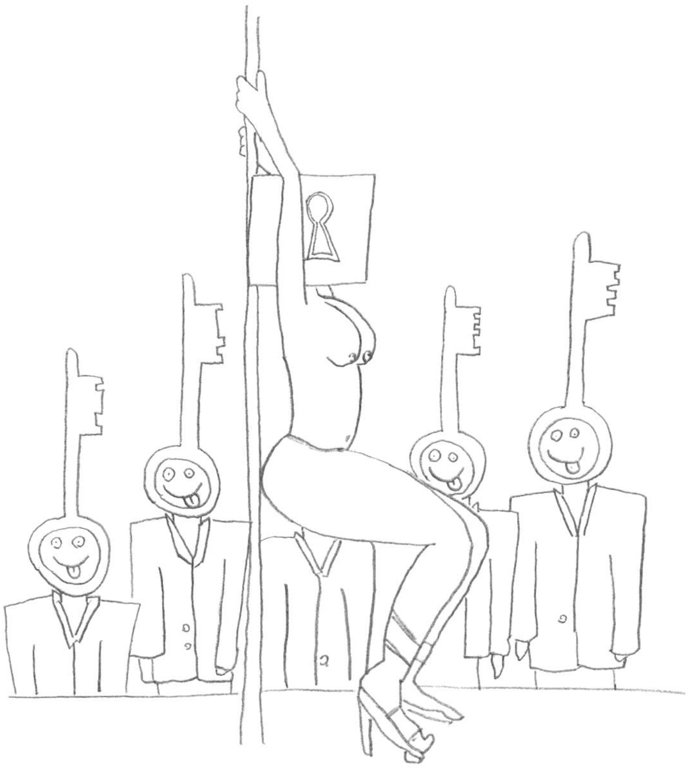

Keys and Lock
2007

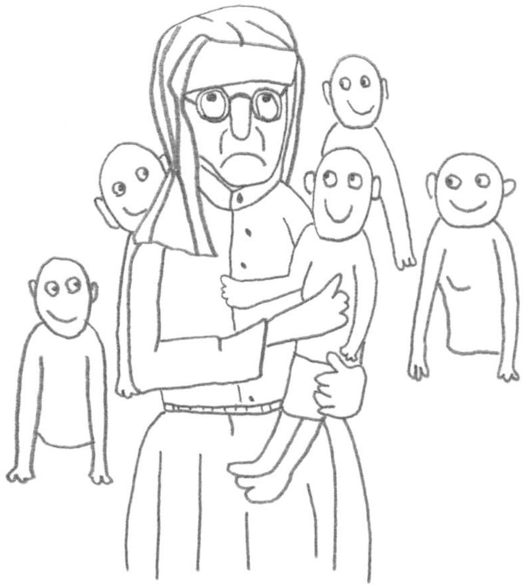

Mother T.
2011

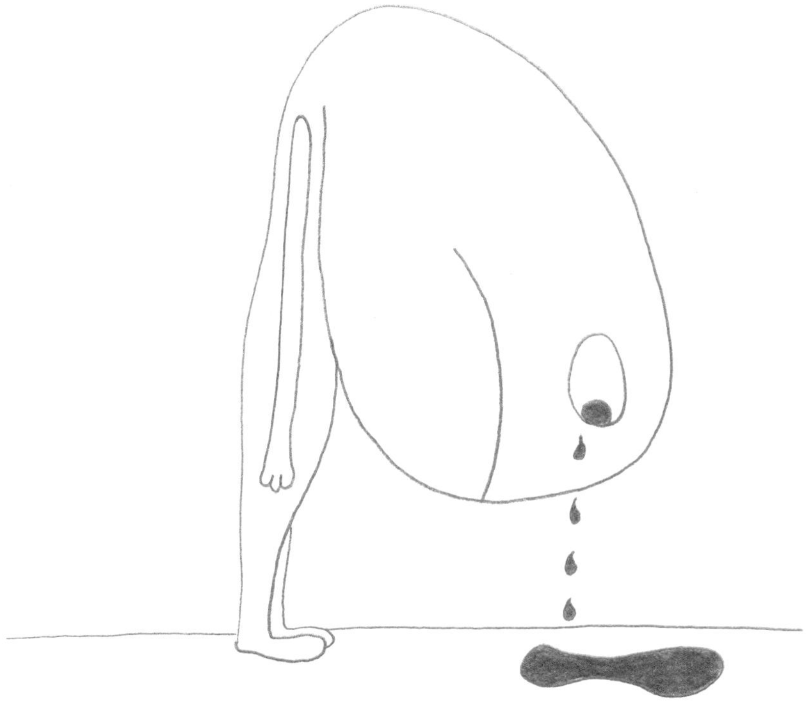

Sady
2015

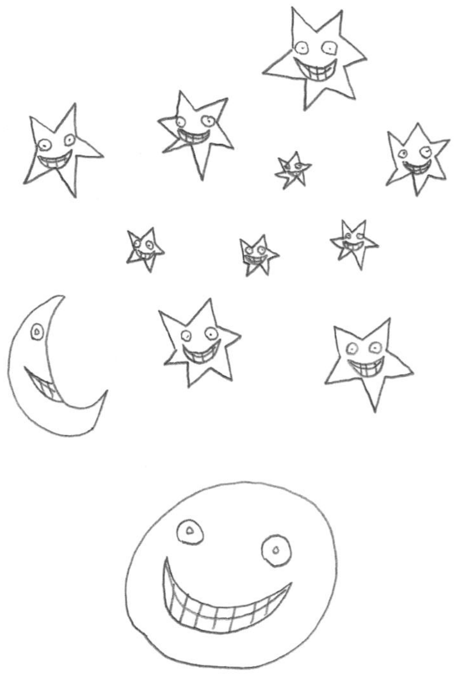

Stars Always Smile
2005

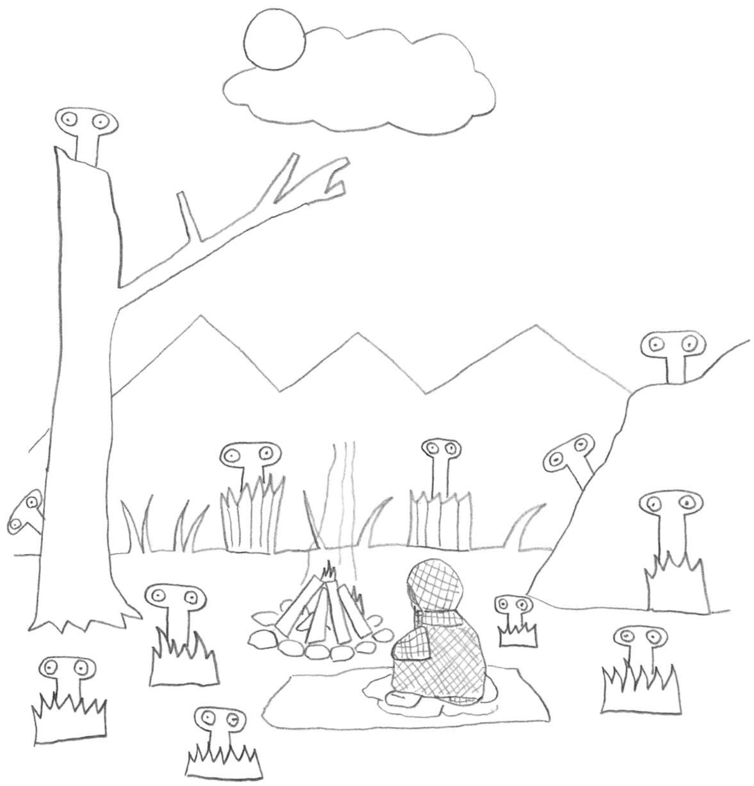

Thriller
2005

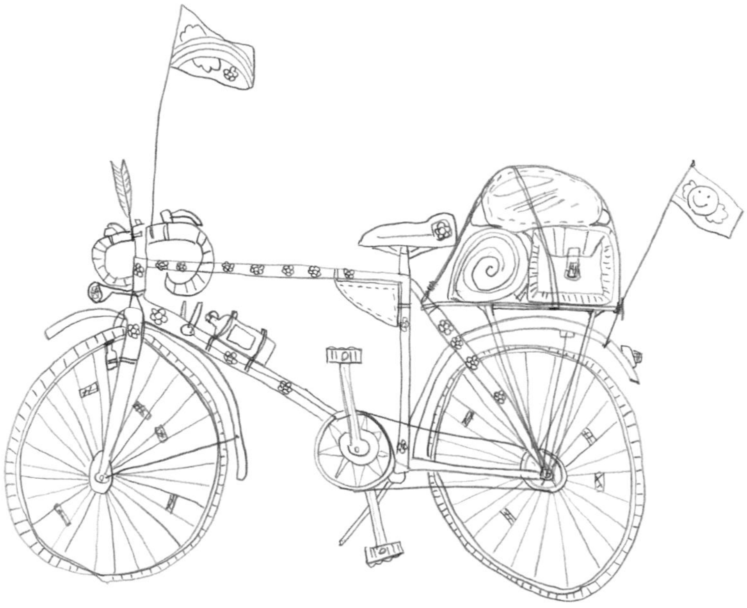

Mein altes Fahrrad
2005

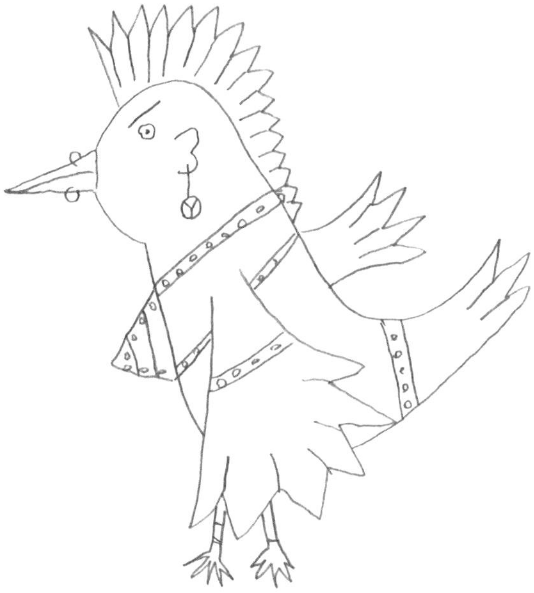

Punk Bird
2007

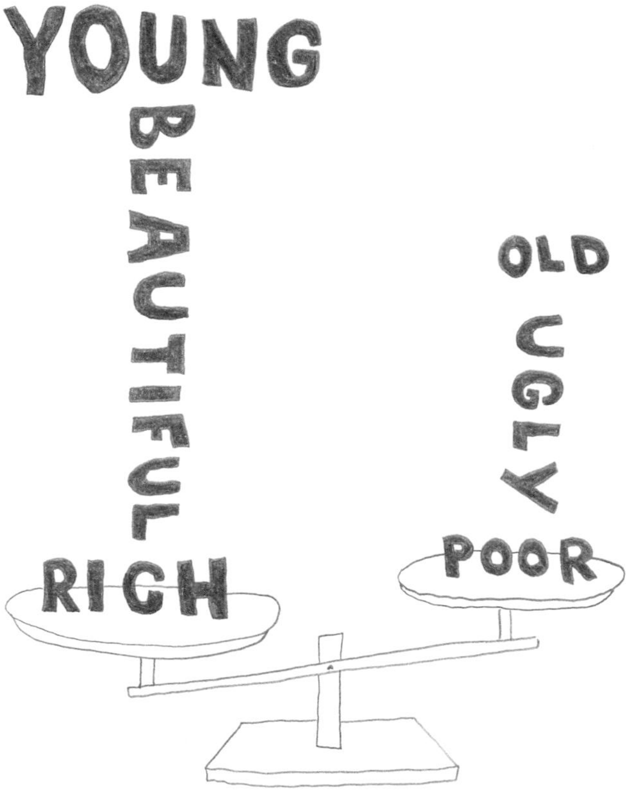

Young and Old
2007

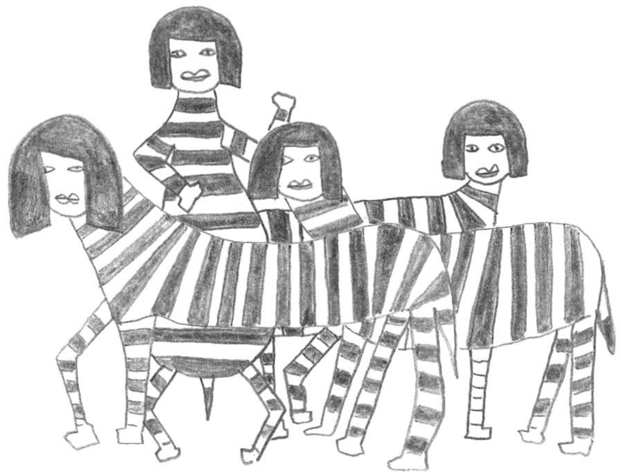

Zebras
2007

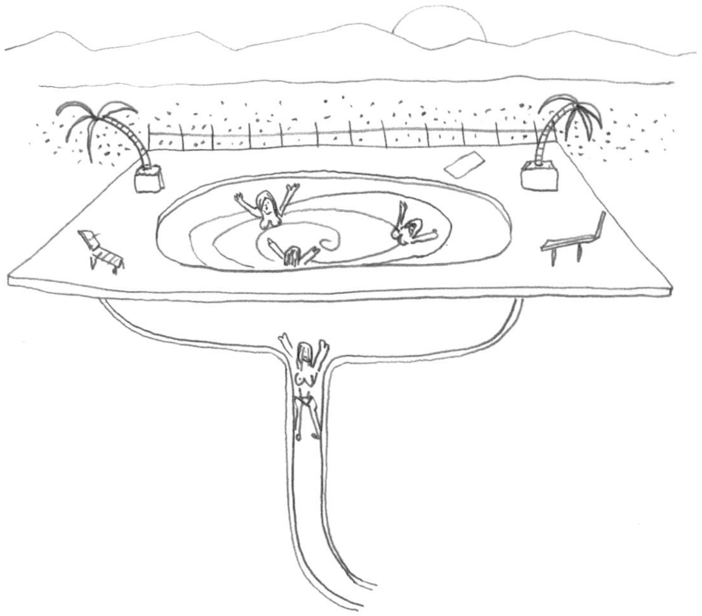

Hollywood Girls
2007

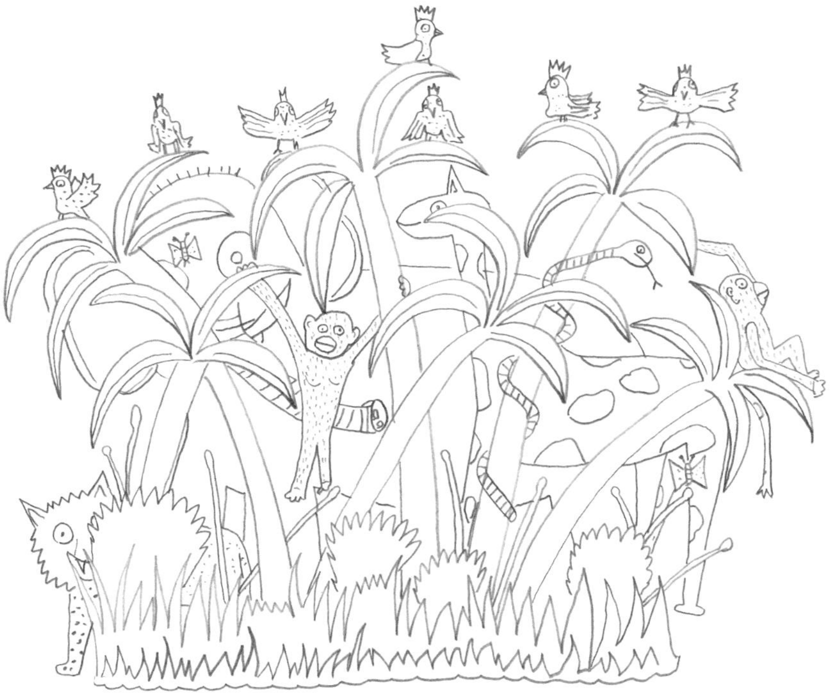

Jungle
2005

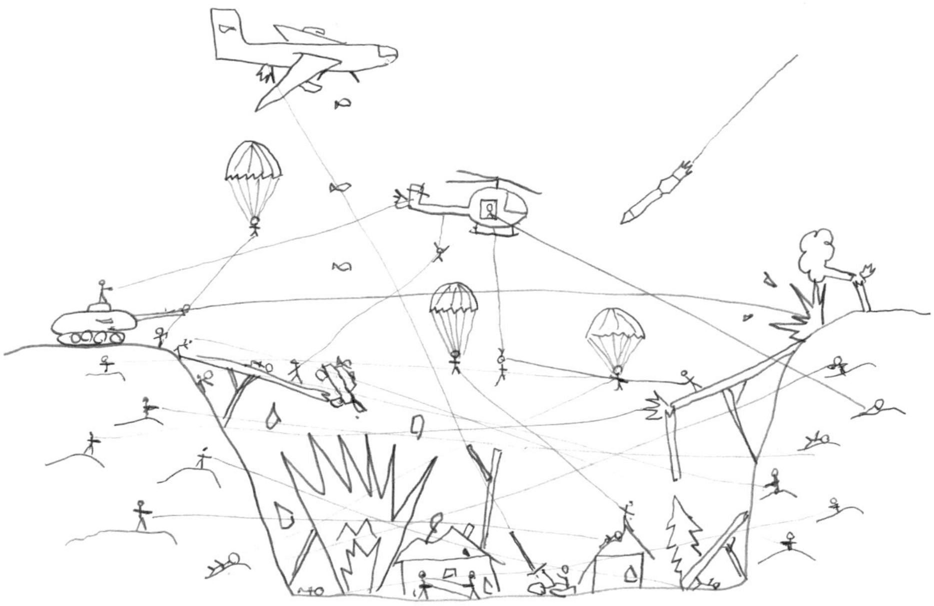

War
2009

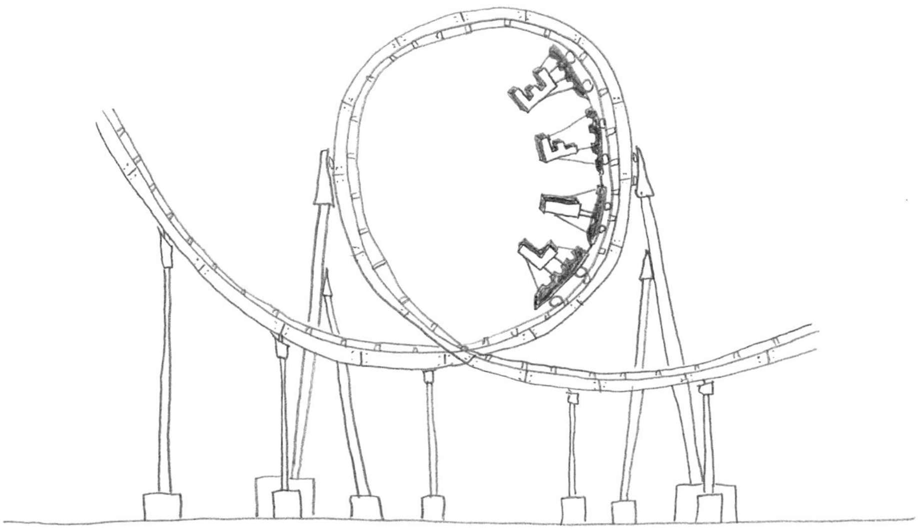

Life Is a Rollercoaster
2007

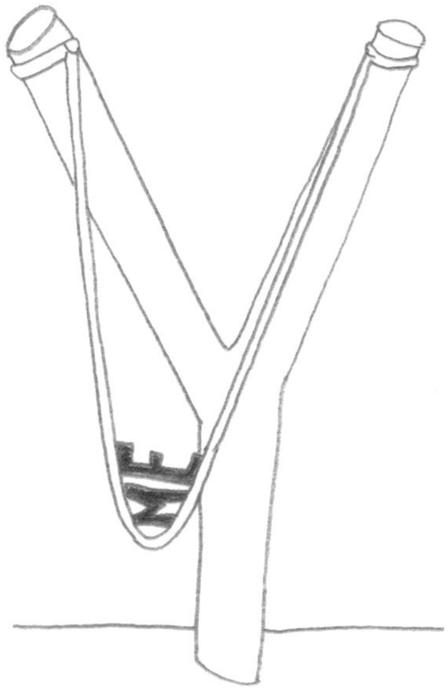

Me
2015

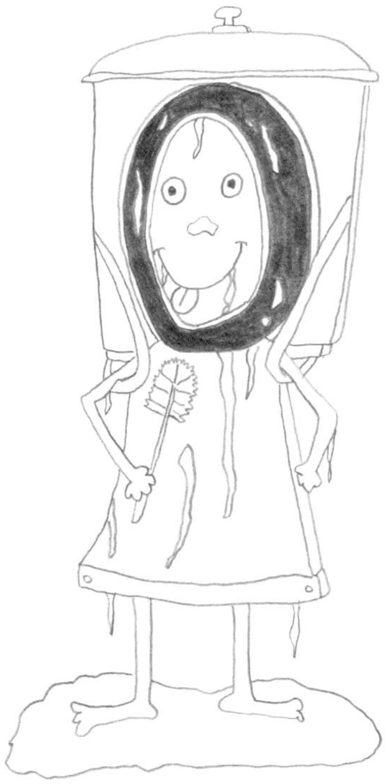

My Dirty Small Brother
2005

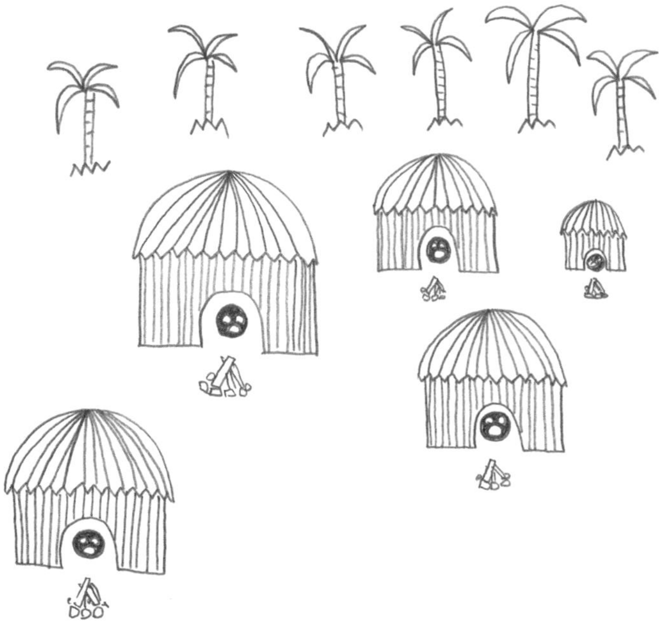

Natives
2007

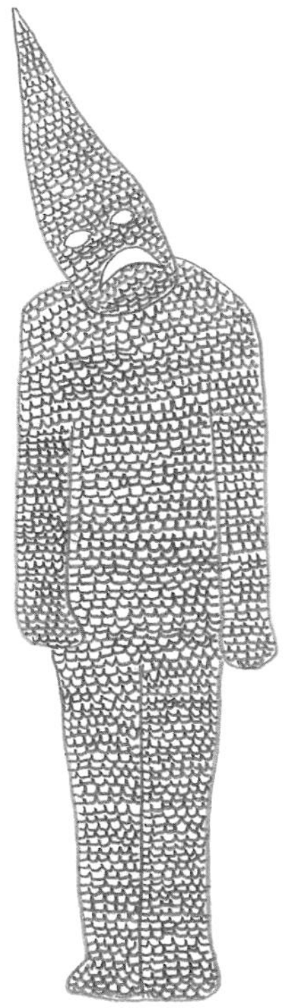

Old House
2005

Just Look at Them, Shut Up, and Think About Them

A discussion about drawing between

Olaf Breuning **and** Brett Littman

on August 8th, 2016

Littman: Olaf, when did you start to draw? Did you draw as a child?

Breuning: As a child, I would say, I was very normal. I did not have any special artistic talent. I guess my parents would say, "Oh, he is making very nice drawings" to be kind. My sister, on the other hand, she was very talented and artistic at an early age.

Early on did you have interest in art? Did you go to a lot of museums?

My parents were more interested in music and other things than in art. They did take me to concerts but not so many museums. I would say that my real interest in art began at the age of 17 when my father gave me a camera and showed me how to develop in the darkroom. From that day on I became a kind of different person. I started to work on my own photo projects and slowly it just seemed like there was no other option for me than to become an artist.

It is interesting to hear that it was photography that influenced you to become an artist. My father was an amateur photographer. He named me after Edward Weston's son—Brett Weston. I grew up with a lot of photo books, cameras and with access to a darkroom. I liked taking pictures. I guess my whole frame of reference early on for art was photography. In retrospect, I think that this really helped me to understand what it means to look at things. Looking through a camera is a way of organizing the world—somewhat analogous to the way drawing helps us to organize the world.

Photographs generally want to show something about the world. To achieve this you look into that world through a frame and you compose your unique story. This for me is close to the way I draw. My drawings are not abstract. They mostly try to say something about the facts of life. I trained my eye as a photographer which meant that I look at something, try to understand it, and then present it as a two-dimensional image.

Did you ever try to make a drawing using a camera-less technique like a photogram?

Yes, I have. I always felt that the photogram was the closest relationship that photography had to drawing or painting. But probably the biggest reason why I became a photographer was that I knew as a child I could never really make a drawing of a horse or anything at all. The moment I had a camera, I knew that world was in front of me, I could use it as I liked and what I made of it people could understand.

It seems to me that over the past decade there has been an implosion of drawing into your photography. In works like Marilyn 10, 2010**, the subjects have colored faces and colored hair, which reads like it was crudely drawn onto them after the photo. As well, in** Protesters**, 2014, the subject's bodies are painted gray and their legs are painted with red and white stripes. In** It's a Man's World, **2008, which is a reproduction of the**

famous photo of modern architects at the 1931 Beaux-Arts Architects annual ball, the subjects wear hand-drawn costumes of iconic buildings. A more recent image that comes to mind is Emojis, 2014, **where your subject's faces are covered by emoticons. Can you talk about the interplay between photography and drawing in your work?**

First of all, I want to tell how happy I was to learn about emojis. They are right up my alley. They are very simple signs that explain emotions. I always try to work with things that are important today and incorporate them into my work. It is interesting what you are saying about photography and drawing in my work—in my early photographs, I would put someone in a fake muscle chest and add long black hair to accentuate some simple idea and show it in powerful stereotypical language ...

Well, it is almost a pre-Photoshop caricature. In a way, instead of manipulating the image in post-production, you actually constructed the image in real time by using drawing, body painting, or costumes.

Yes, I guess what ties it all together is that I am trying to use simple gestures to explore the figurative—and for me drawing is the way I can achieve this. I am not a complicated guy, and I am not a complicated artist.

You started making drawings 15 years ago?

Yes, more or less. I have been drawing regularly and showing my drawings for about 12 to 13 years now.

Your drawing practice is very regimented. I know that you used to draw at Balthazar, a restaurant in SoHo, where you would go every morning for breakfast. You would have a specific kind of notebook and the B2 pencil that you use to make your drawings. You also did a series of drawings on the Queen Mary during two cruises from NY to the UK. Why do you need this kind of structure to draw?

Well, in the beginning of my career I did not take drawing seriously as an art medium. I generally used drawings as plans for my photographs. I would make very detailed drawings for my very complicated big photographs. The drawing was practically the photograph. All of a sudden, I looked at these drawings more seriously and people around me started to look at them too and think that they were pretty cute and good—and that encouraged me.

However, for me sitting in front of a blank piece of paper with a pen alone in a studio is not a good way to work. I set up a very beautiful table upstate where I live that looks out to a panoramic view of the Catskills and thought that is going to be the place to make drawings. I have tried many times to sit there but nothing happened. I had to find that place where I can focus on drawing—a busy place like Balthazar or on the Queen Mary—where I could observe people and generate ideas.

I like people. I want to tell stories about humans and the tragedy of life. I feel a lot of empathy for the worldview of someone like Woody Allen or Larry David. I am a very optimistic person, but at the same time I want to deal with things that are kind of sad like death and war. When I am in Balthazar and I see a waitress serving something, I might have an idea of someone serving food in a French maid costume, then all of a sudden my brain starts to work.

The thing is that I fish for ideas. I look out there and I see certain things, and suddenly one small idea pops into my head and I try to take that idea and turn it into a snowball that starts an avalanche. Sometimes it works, sometimes it doesn't.

When I have a successful drawing session I am pretty sure that in my case it has a lot to do with my neurobiological state of mind, you know? Sometimes I am just enthusiastic and stuff just floats out, and sometimes I just sit in Balthazar and try to make a drawing and make a circle and then nothing more happens. One thing I have noticed is after having about two or three cups of coffee my brain really starts to hum and ideas flow better. Once I got a prescription for that focus drug Ritalin to see if it would help me. It was a total disaster. I was in my studio and I would look at a wall, and then I would see something wrong with the wall and become totally lost and obsessed with a crack or something. I could not really focus on drawing at all. It is too bad the Ritalin didn't work—I really hoped it was going to—I would have been a much more efficient artist. Right now I can only make about 20 drawings every three to four months.

Can you talk about how the drawings in your notebooks are later elaborated onto the A4 sheets of paper?

I often review my notebook drawings to see what is good and what is not good. Once I determine a sketch or idea from the book is good, I sit down and try and make the drawing on the larger A4 paper. I do not use an eraser and my drawings are generally made with one continuous line, so it can take a couple of tries to make it perfect. Once I have a perfect drawing, I scan it into my computer and then it becomes accepted into my family of drawings and then its life begins. That drawing can be printed on T-shirts, bags, drawn large on the wall in an exhibition, or printed in a book. As you can imagine, I have a lot of drawings that do not make it into the family—they are just hanging around waiting for their adoption.

What is interesting to me is that aesthetically your drawings present themselves as immediate. I do not think that anyone really knows that your drawings have been refined three or four times before they are done. I thought that maybe you just ripped a page out of your notebook and you scanned it. My assumption was that you can sit down and make a beautiful and perfectly rendered drawing in your style at any given time—but obviously that is not the way you work at all.

Well, if I had an idea now I could probably draw it in a couple of minutes with a few tries. My process is still fast—even though there are a couple of steps to get to the completed work. The final drawing is still like a one-minute drawing. Sometimes, and it is very rare, I make a drawing in my notebook that is perfect. In that case I take the drawing and try to trace it exactly onto the A4 paper by putting it up against a window. But it still remains a quick drawing. I really wish I would be so talented that I could just have blank pages and just toss off great drawings one after another… next, next, next. Unfortunately, I am more like a squirrel that collects nuts for the winter. I collect all of my ideas in the notebooks and they need to sustain me for a long time.

So you go back to your notebooks to look for ideas?

Well, yes and no. The notebooks are both springboards for ideas and their death. I am 46 years old now and I have been working as a professional artist for 20 years. It is getting more and more difficult for me to produce new works because I always want to do something that I have never done before. When I made a drawing of a guy jumping from a skyscraper with the people with the net on the wrong side of the building that idea was finished for me. I could never make a similar drawing with that same image because I have seen that idea and now it is done.

So you are not the kind of artist who is going to go back and look at the drawing of the guy jumping off the wrong side of the building and redraw that from 25 different angles. The idea is there. It is done, and you cannot really go back.

This is why I might be described as a restless artist who works in many mediums. You mentioned the emoji photo earlier; I will never do another work with emojis. The only things that stay consistent in my work are the bigger issues like sexuality, death, and violence.

Ok, but you do continue to make drawings. What is it about this medium that is useful to you in your artistic practice other than to make an idea physically present?

Lately, I feel that I have developed a kind of a language in my drawings, but I would have to go to a shrink to explain what that language is! Look, there are a lot of other artists that really care about the skill and craft of drawing more than I do. For me the medium of drawing is a tool to explain complex ideas very simply.

Why, for you, is drawing the best way to explore these deeper philosophical ideas?

Well, I feel I am trying to explore those things as well in all of the mediums that I work with, especially in my films and in my photographs. But with drawings I can explain something about the human condition very simply. I really like flipping through the mock-up of this catalog and seeing the 232 drawings again. For me it has become a great and fast way of going through the inventory of my life, certain events and my thoughts at specific times.

Let's look at one specific drawing—the one where the bomb is falling on the tank, the tank is shooting another person who in turn is shooting another person with a gun who is killing a fly. To me this drawing confronts our daily existence through a violent story. We always try to use our intellect and morals to explain certain things and sometimes that just fails. When someone is killed by an axe murderer on a train we ask, "Why did that person do it?" I can try and analyze their motives but sometimes the act is just beyond comprehension.

In my drawing of this violent chain reaction I feel that I am not explaining why these situations happen but I am putting down an anchor for myself into the situation and looking for some clarity.

Well, clarity is one of the more radical positions one can take. I think your drawings are clear. They are very simple and there is not much to take in. I look at the drawing of the bus with the kids dangling on the edge of the cliff and I immediately understand the binary of life and death. I do not think there could be anyone who would see that drawing and not understand what the issue is.

Yes, my drawings want to approach clarity. When I make a photograph I have to deal with color, people, the site, the weather—there are so many more things that your brain has to process. The drawing is just so simple. For me it is more precise and direct as opposed to a long explanation of the situation of why the kids in the bus are dangling on the cliff. With drawing I am a monk. With my other mediums I am more manic.

I would say that your wooden sculptures from 2012 seem to share the same kind of simplicity as your drawings. When I first started following your work in 2005 it seemed more about excessive accumulation. You were layering one thing on top of the other on top of the other to a kind of breaking point. The films Home 1, 2, **and** 3 **even border on being unwatchable. The drawings and the simple wooden sculptures seem to be a move away from that accumulative impulse. A more reductive spirit.**

You are completely right. Over the years I have liked layering and putting a lot of stuff together to make a mix. This was very comfortable and second nature to me. It is difficult for me to explain why I wanted to do this. More recently, however, I have enjoyed a more reductive approach to my work. This is not to say that the work is not complex, it is just more stripped down.

Do you view your drawings as political?

This is always a question for an artist—do you really have a mission? I guess at some point artists had a strong feeling that art had to educate people. Today it is a crazier world, a kind of Biblical Babylon—so it kind of doesn't matter if art educates. There is so much art around, who really gives a shit about what it does?

I think the last thing I would want to do is to educate people with my art.

That said, I would be happy to make or give a drawing for a political campaign because I do think that my work is in a way political, since it speaks about very human conditions, and politics are nothing more than that. I mean right now, I think I could make a drawing that could narrow down what the Clinton/Trump election is all about. In the end, art is my way of going through life. If I didn't have art my life would be more difficult.

A lot of people talk about the humor in your work. I think that humor for you is closer to slapstick and vaudeville than irony—is it a way for you to collapse taboos and accentuate stereotypes?

I do like humor. In my films and photography, I might be using humor to poke and prod people more about their received ideas. In my drawings, however, I want people to just look at them, shut up, and think about them. More recently, I have been trying to be more honest and real. I just want to be straightforward and honest. I feel that this is the best way for me to make art now.

Olaf, I have been following you on Instagram and have been giving some thought to the idea that your feed is a kind of drawing practice for you. It is one of the mediums that you have used where you have taken a sustained look at one thing—the face.

Hmm, for me Instagram is a place for low-level intelligence images. You know I make the faces from food and found objects. I don't give a lot of thought to them. But I guess other people do.

I get a lot of comments like: "Why don't you make a coffee table book with them?" This kind of horrifies me. I mean I like the idea and I am sure it would be popular but I did have the thought that Instagram might be the only thing I would be remembered for as an artist. That would be kind of sad and funny at the same time.

Why do you think you keep focusing on the abstract of the face as the subject for your feed?

Since I started my feed in December 2013 with a picture of moss, a leaf, and some twigs that kind of looked like a bunny with its tongue out, I have posted hundreds of images on Instagram and I have many thousand followers, whatever that means. I really just collect these faces with my iPhone. Most of these images are right there in front of me. Sometimes I just add a little something to them. I guess like with my drawings I see a language developing in these images that connect up to other themes in my work. The face is such a simple thing to express and personalize. You just need the basics: eyes, hair, mouths.

What makes a drawing successful for you? Does the horizon of success for you end with you just being satisfied with the drawing or the drawing communicating something specific?

Being satisfied with the drawing personally is where the horizon of success ends for me. I really don't show my drawings to many people before I exhibit them. Maybe I show them to my wife Makiko, but I'm not someone who really needs other people's opinions about a work. People can always say whatever they want about my work because we have seven billion people on the planet. One person thinks this and another person thinks that and I am just fine with that.

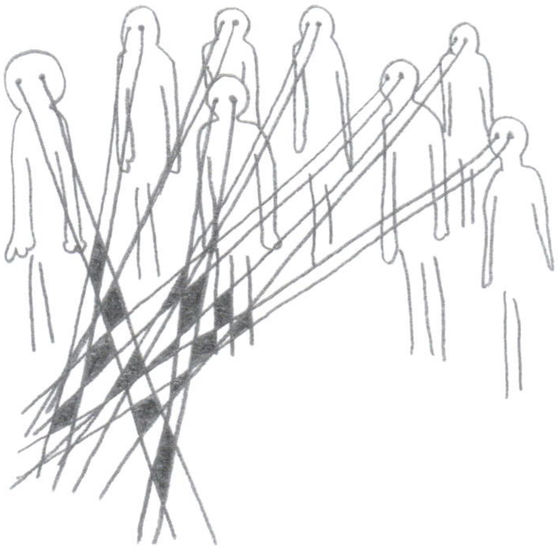

Pattern of Common Sense
2009

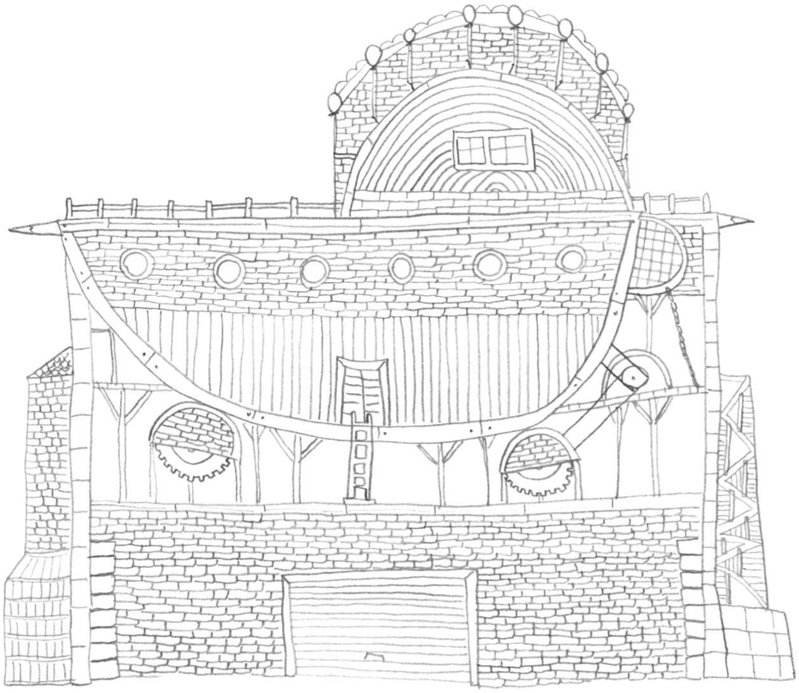

Mother House
2005

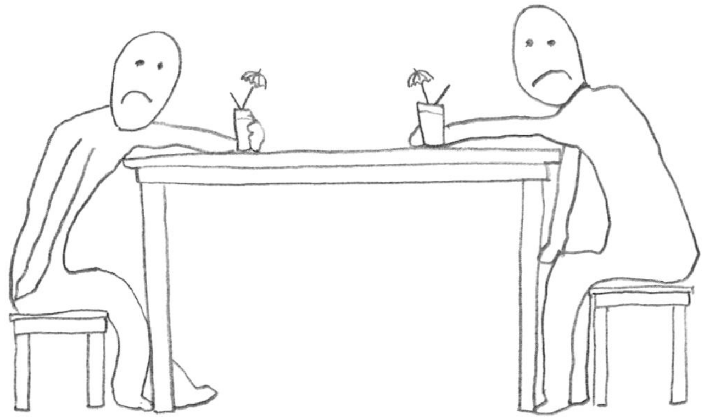

Not Even Drinks Make Us Happy
2009

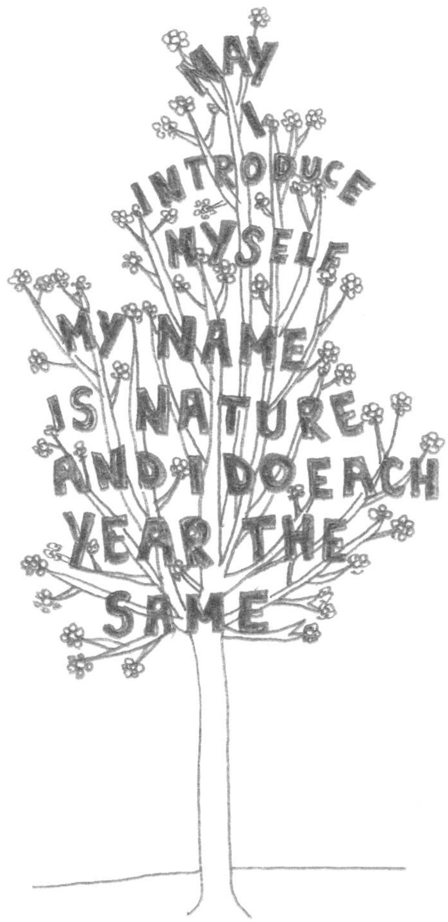

May I Introduce Myself
2014

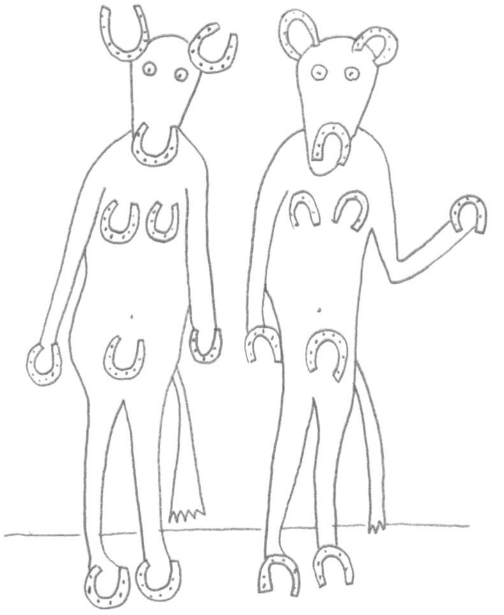

Happy Horse and Unhappy Horse
2012

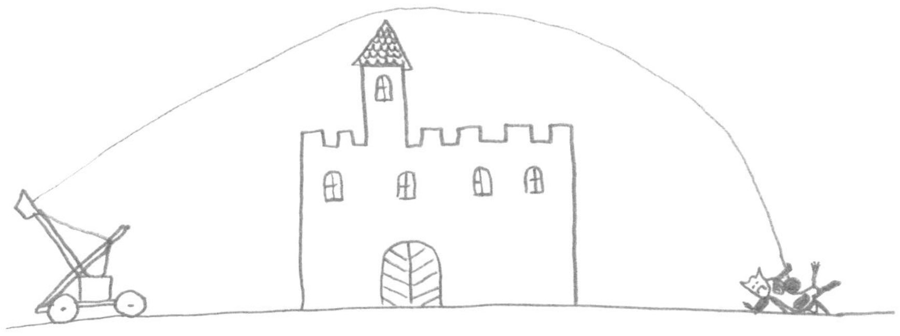

Poor Cow
2011

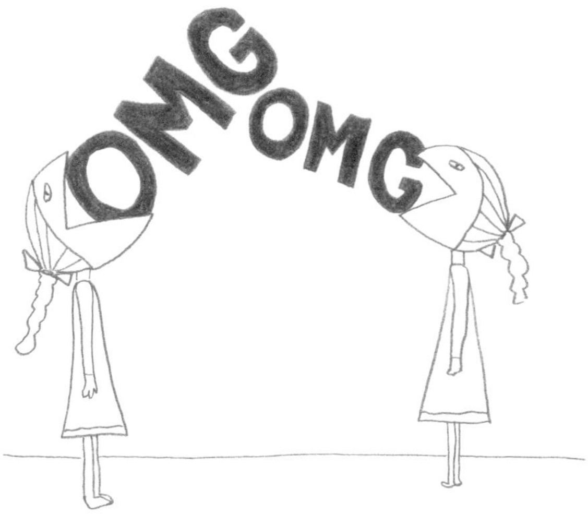

OMG
2013

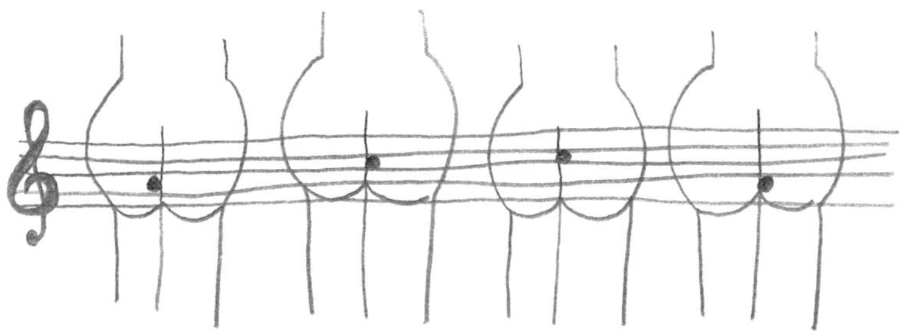

Ass Music
2008

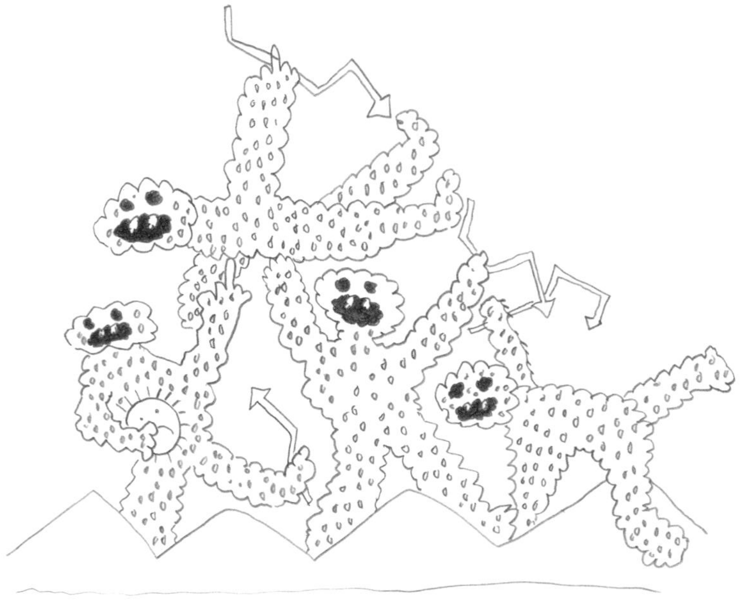

Schlechtes Wetter
2005

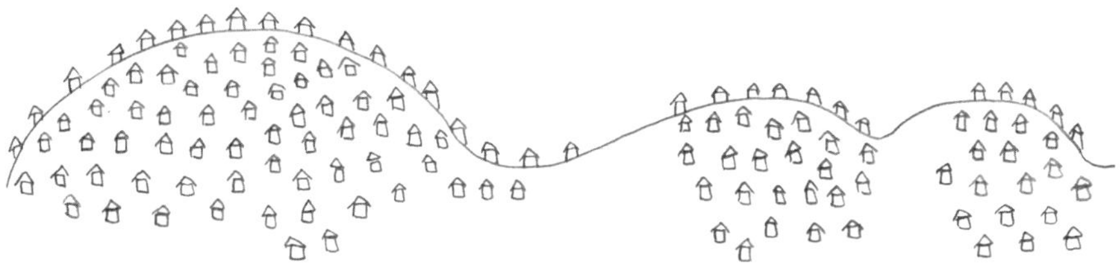

Homes
2008

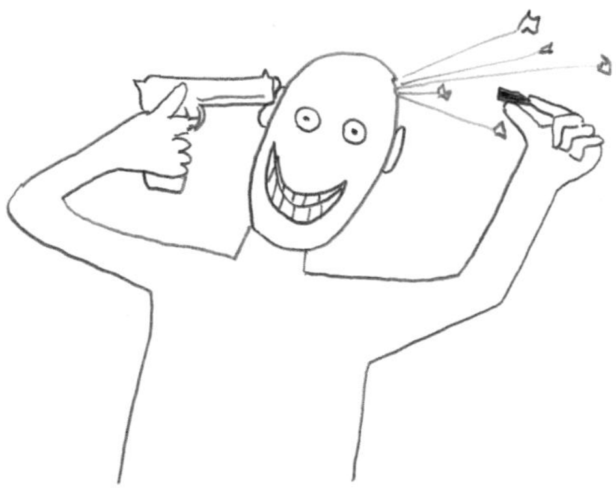

Got It
2005

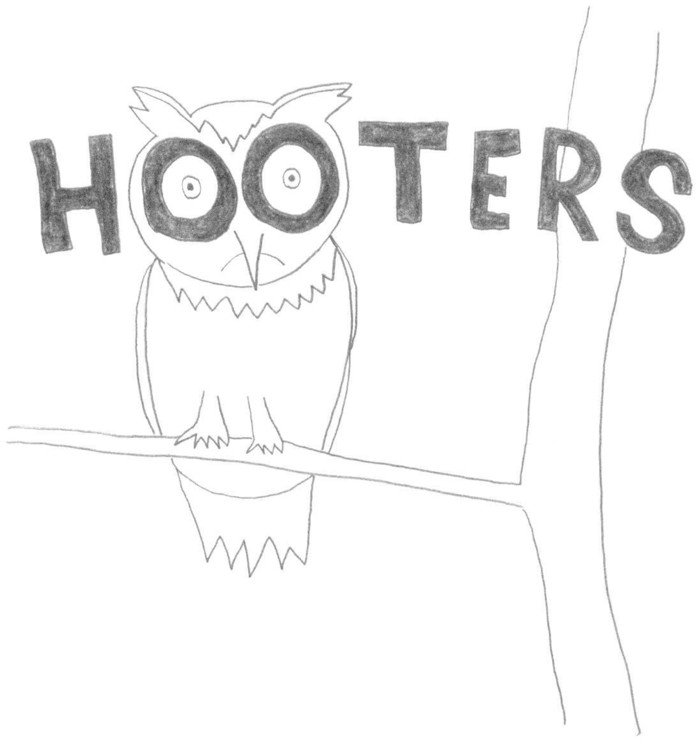

Hooters
2013

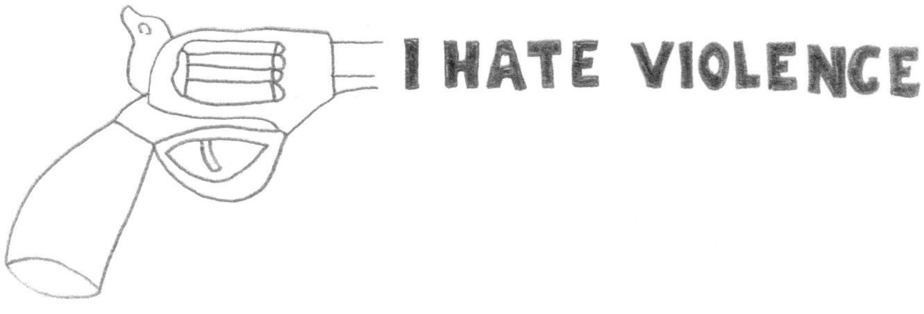

I Hate Violence
2011

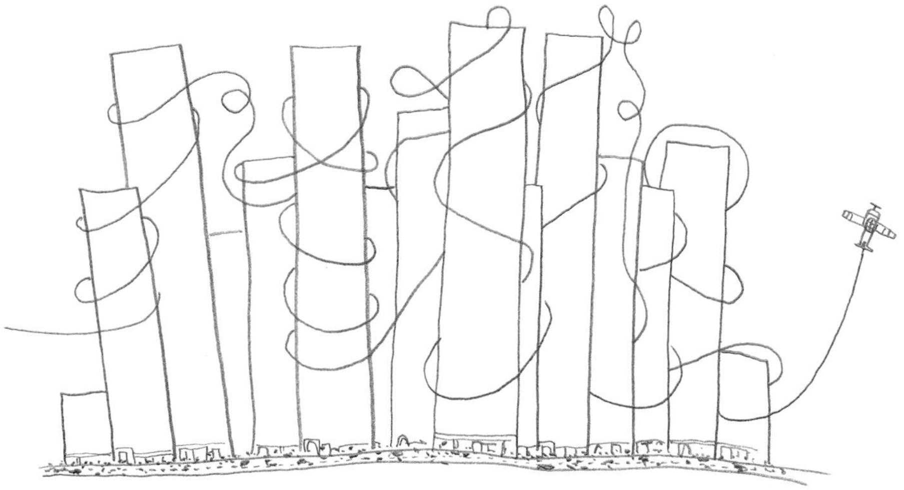

Good Pilot
2010

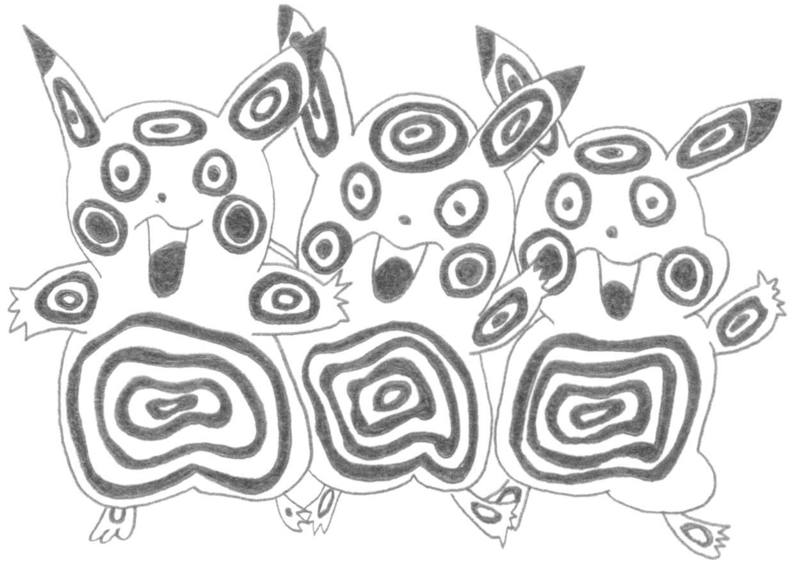

Picky Picky Picky
2011

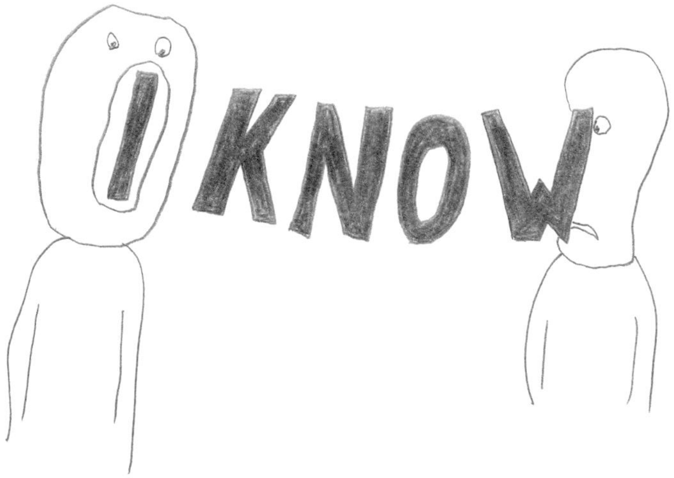

I Know
2010

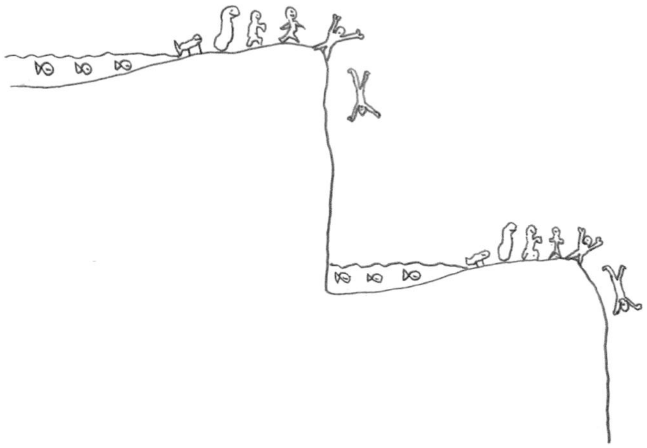

On and on
2007

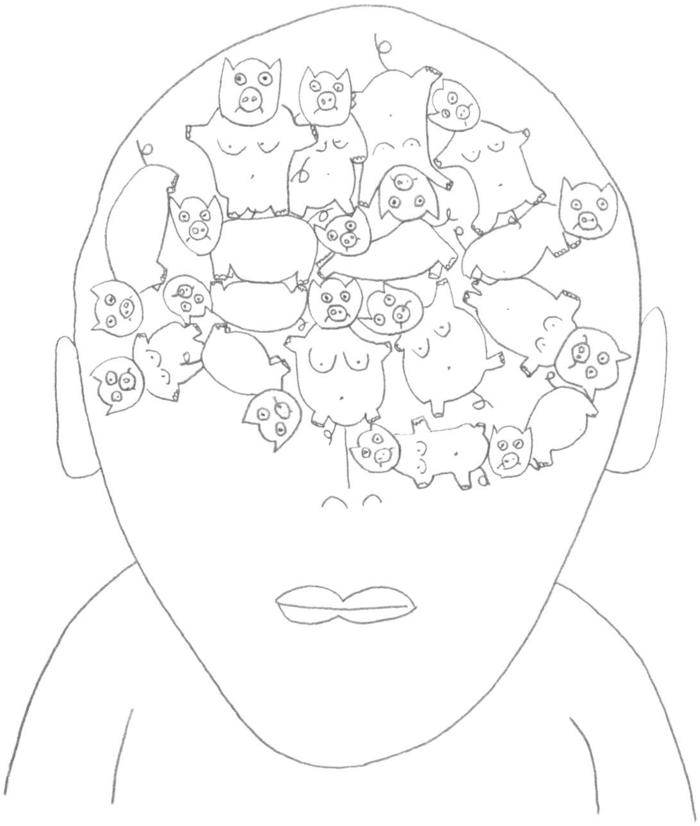

Pigs in My Head
2014

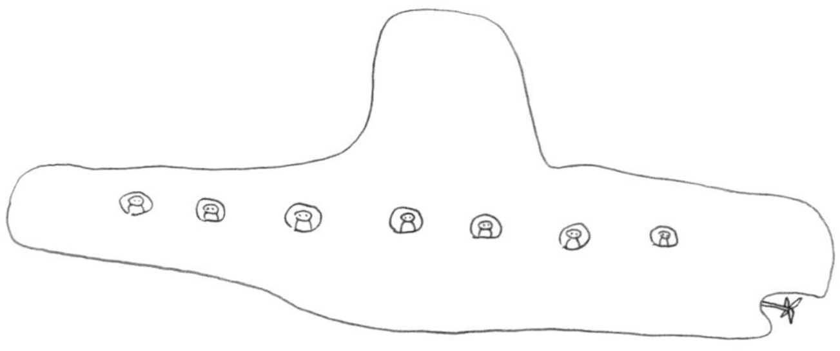

Submarine
2009

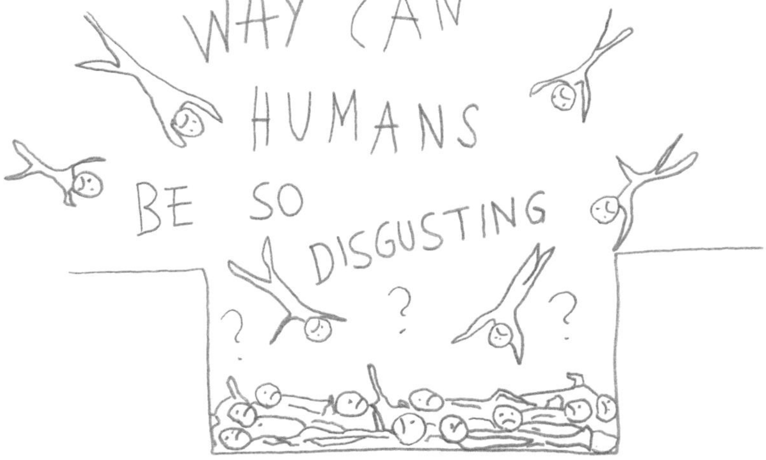

Why Can Humans Be so Disgusting?
2011

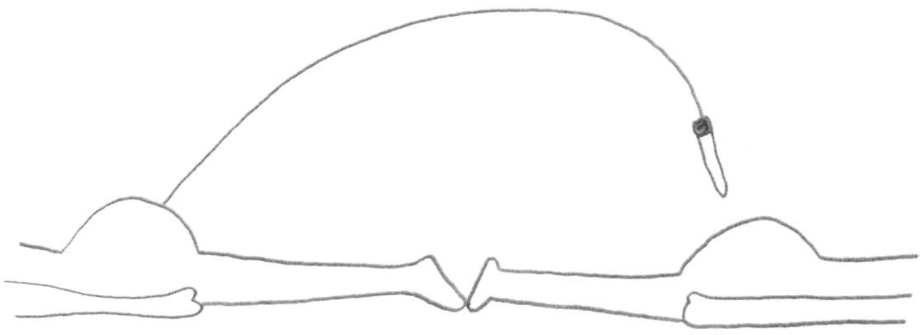

Missile
2012

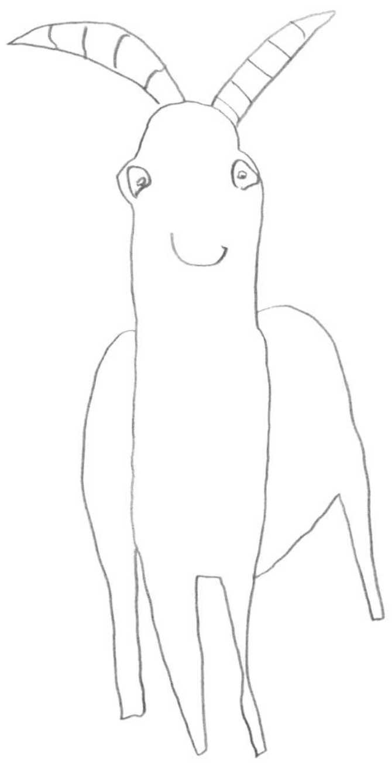

Goat
2005

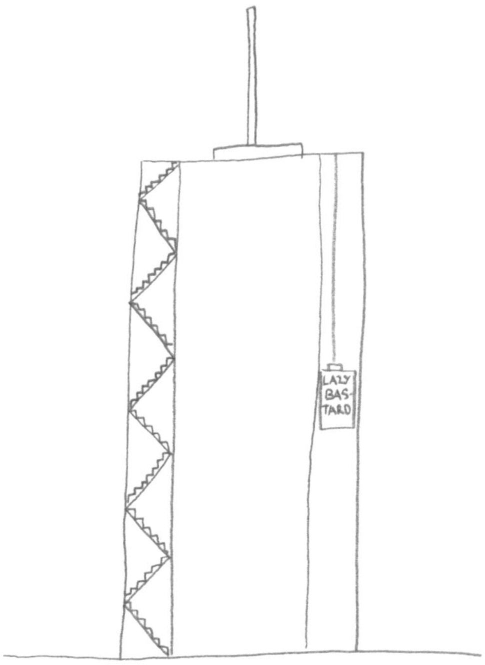

Lazy Bastard
2016

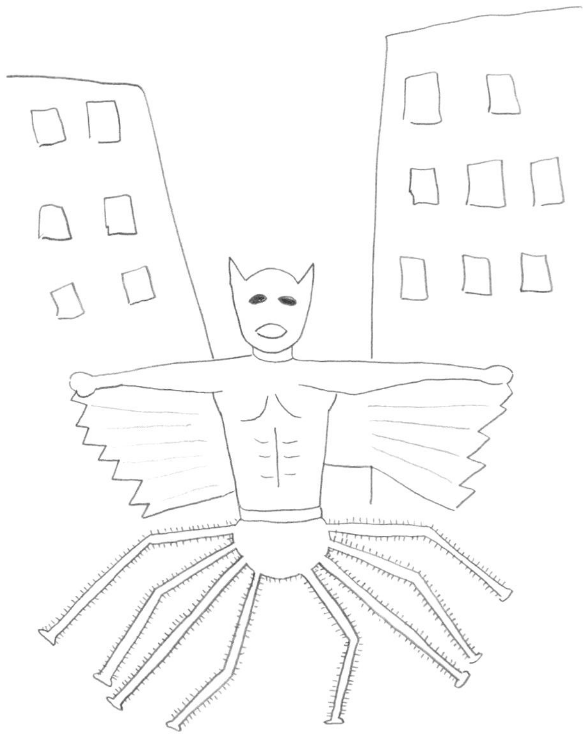

Bat-Spider-Man
2005

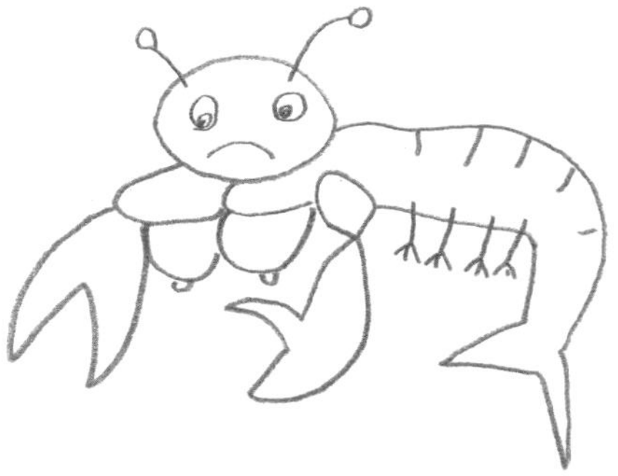

Sexy Lobster
2016

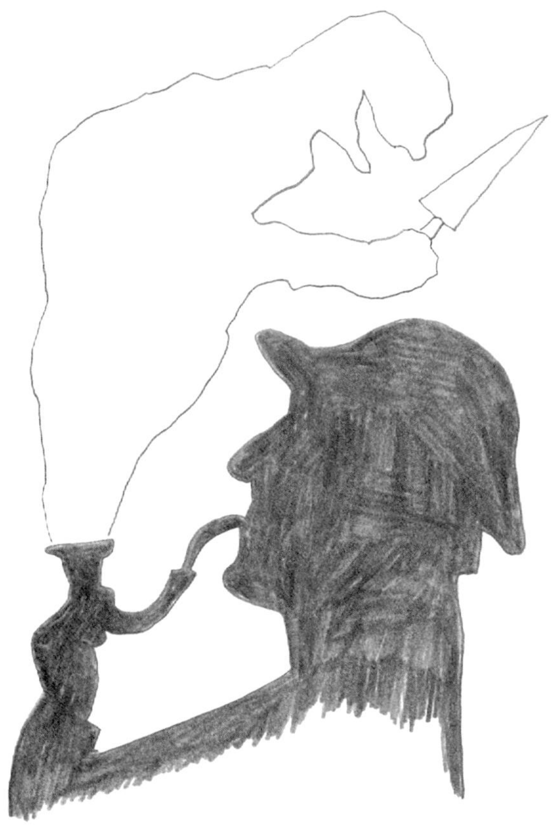

Holmes
2007

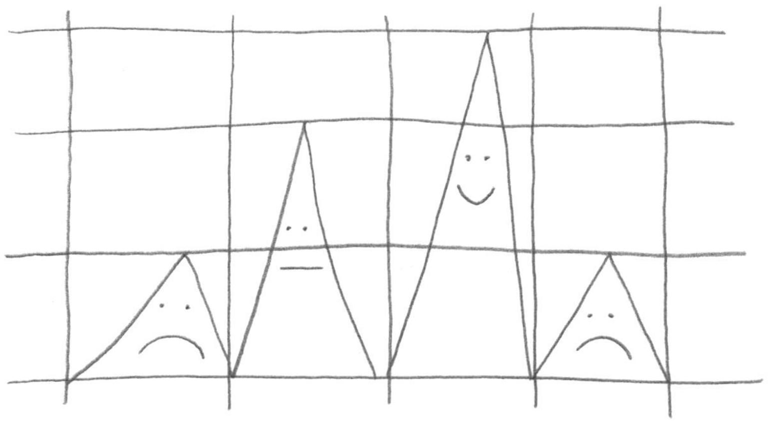

Stock Market
2011

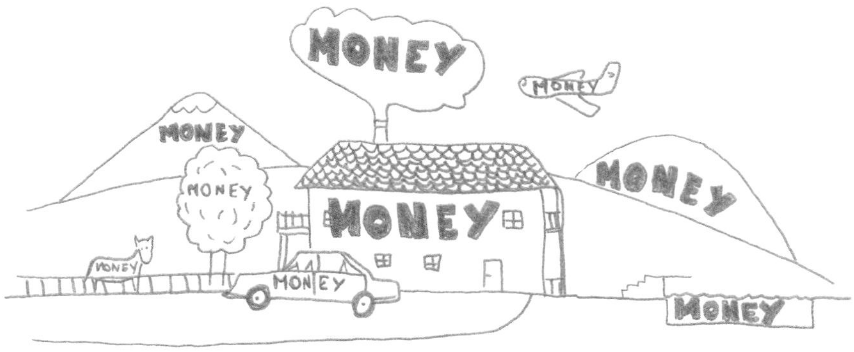

All About the Money
2013

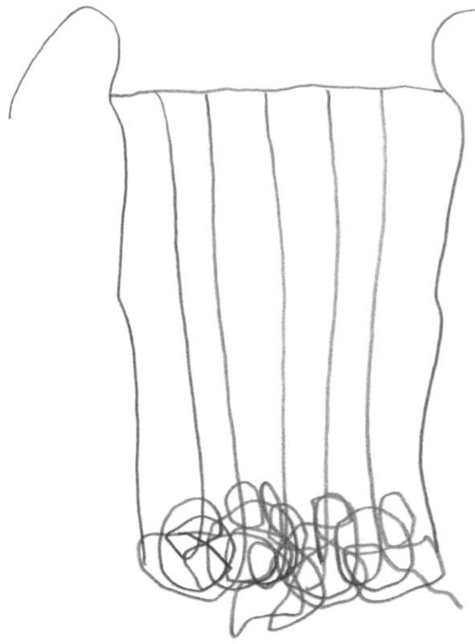

Waterfall
2005

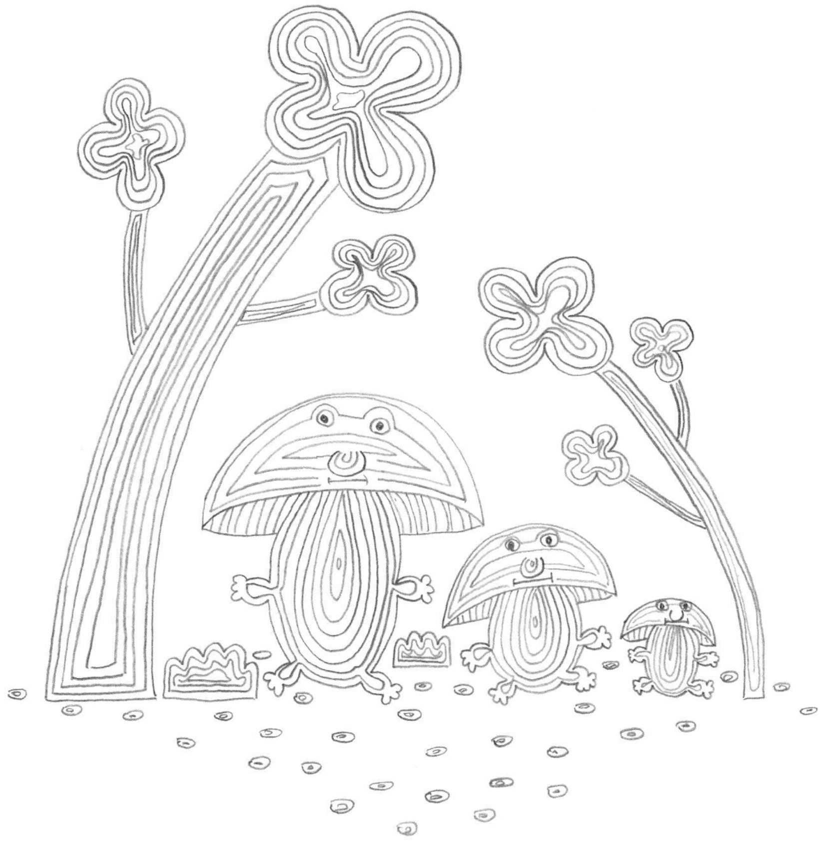

Magic Mushrooms
2005

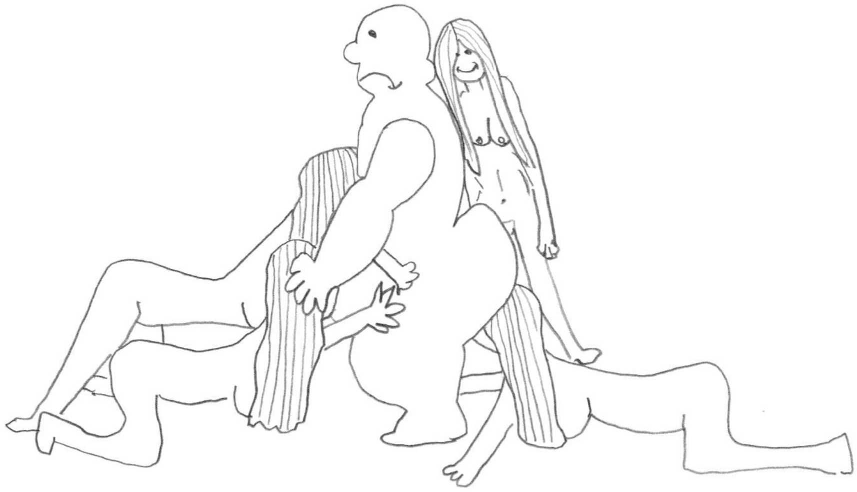

Oh, We Men Want It All so Much!
2005

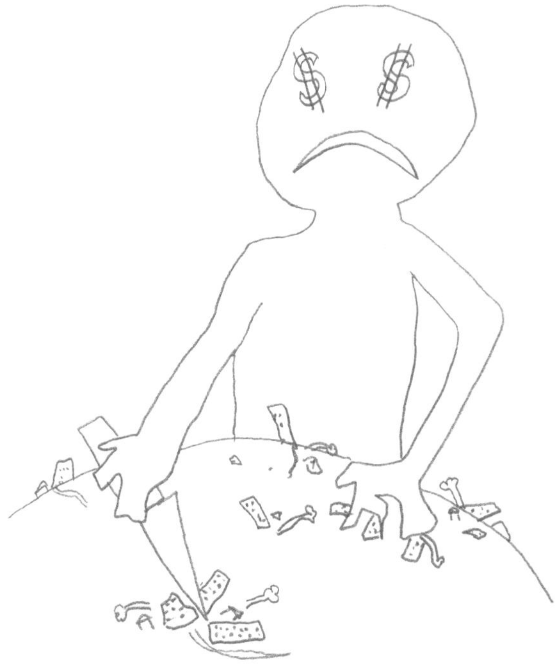

Mr Greedy
2015

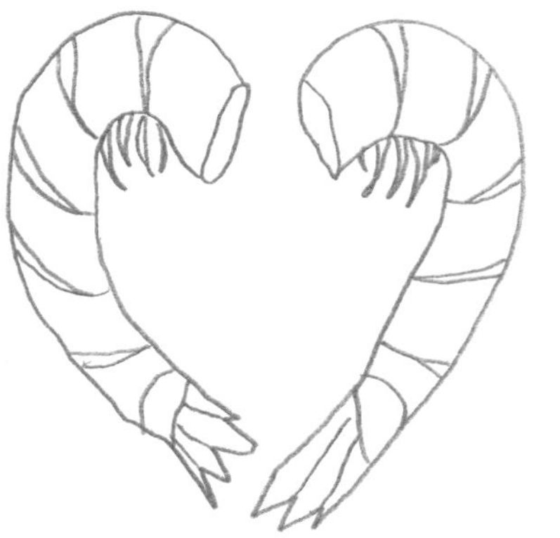

Shrimp Heart
2012

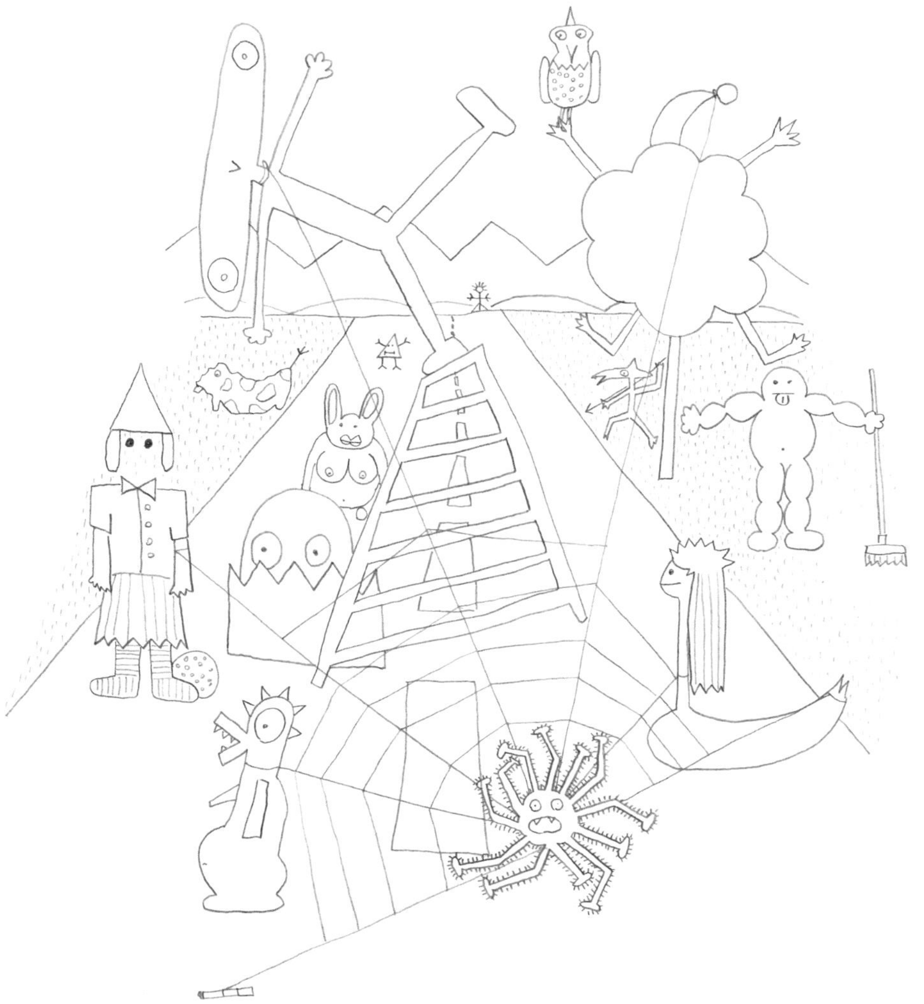

The Angry Spider
2005

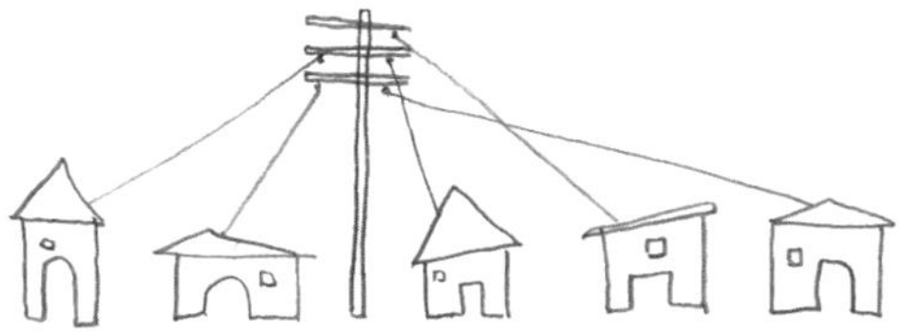

Poor Neighborhood
2007

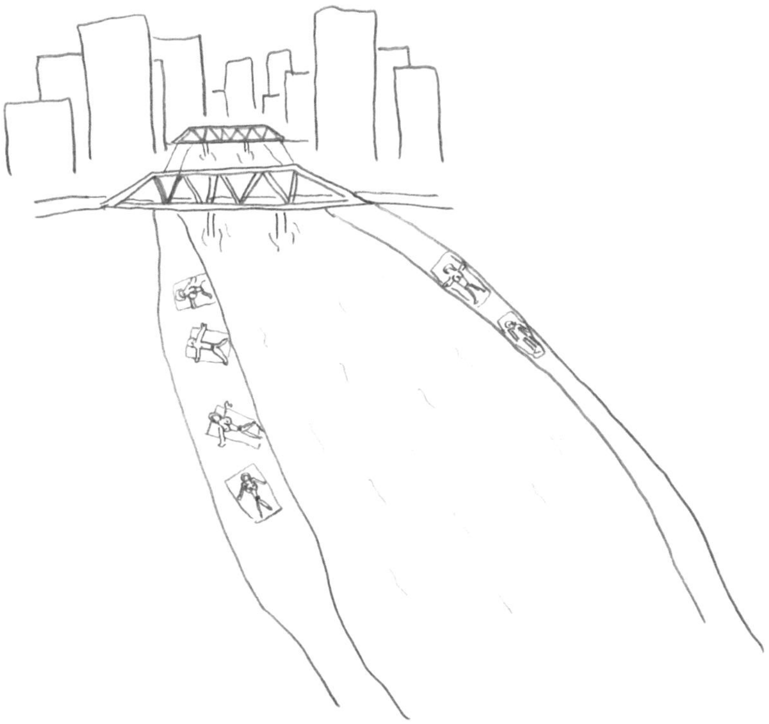

Strand
2010

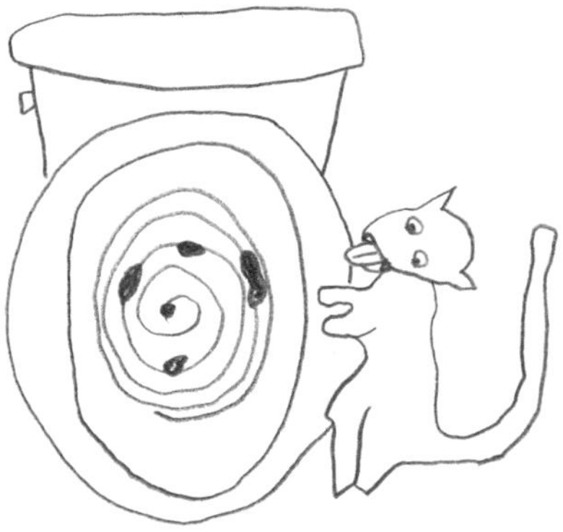

Whale
2009

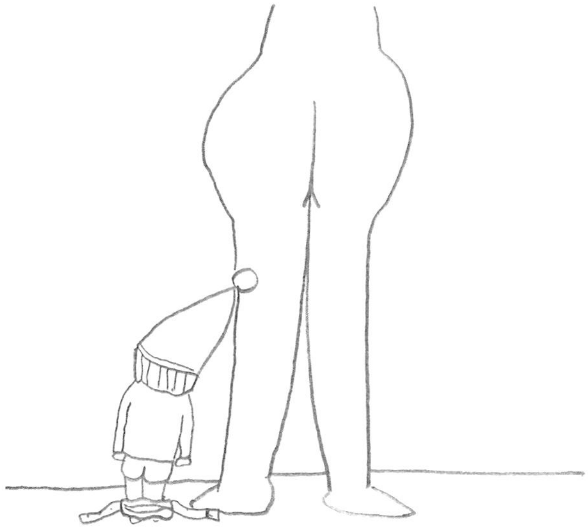

Too Small
2007

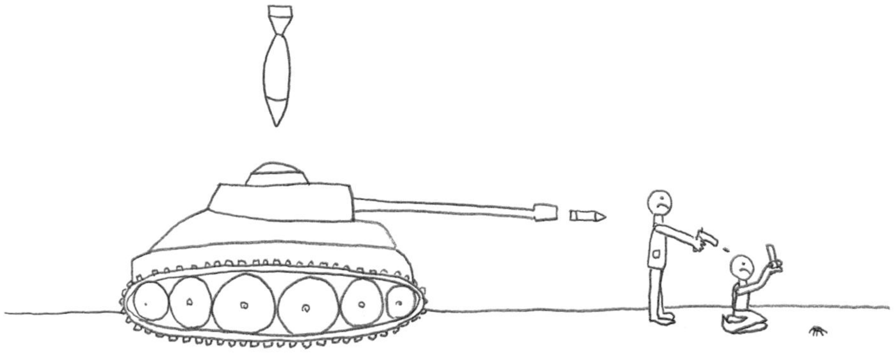

We Are so Violent
2007

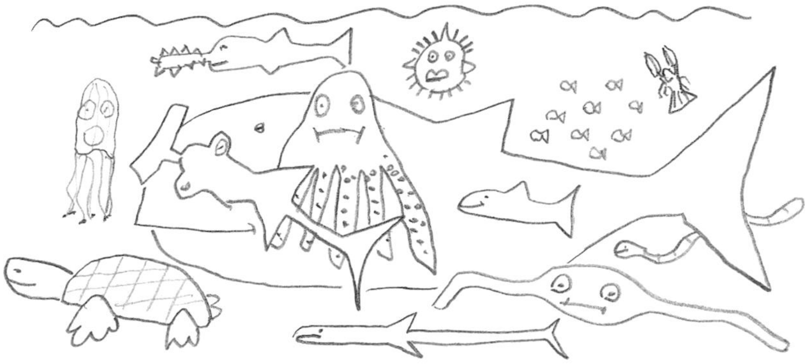

Traffic in the Sea
2005

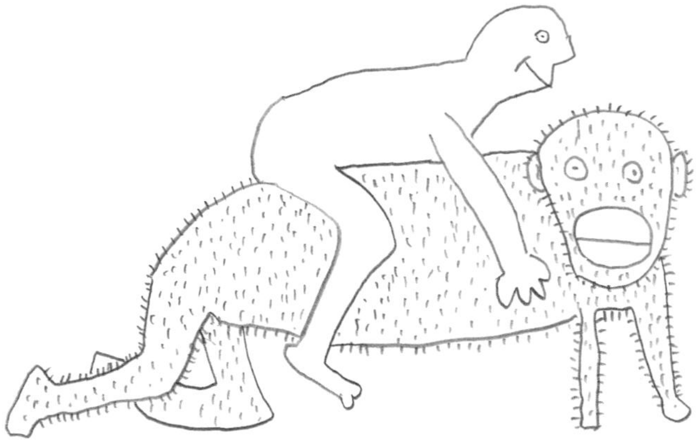

We Have Animals Under Control
2005

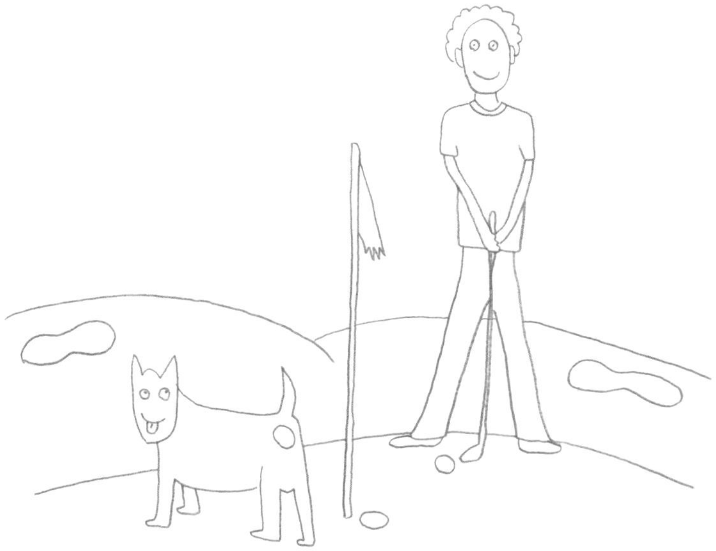

Wrong Hole
2007

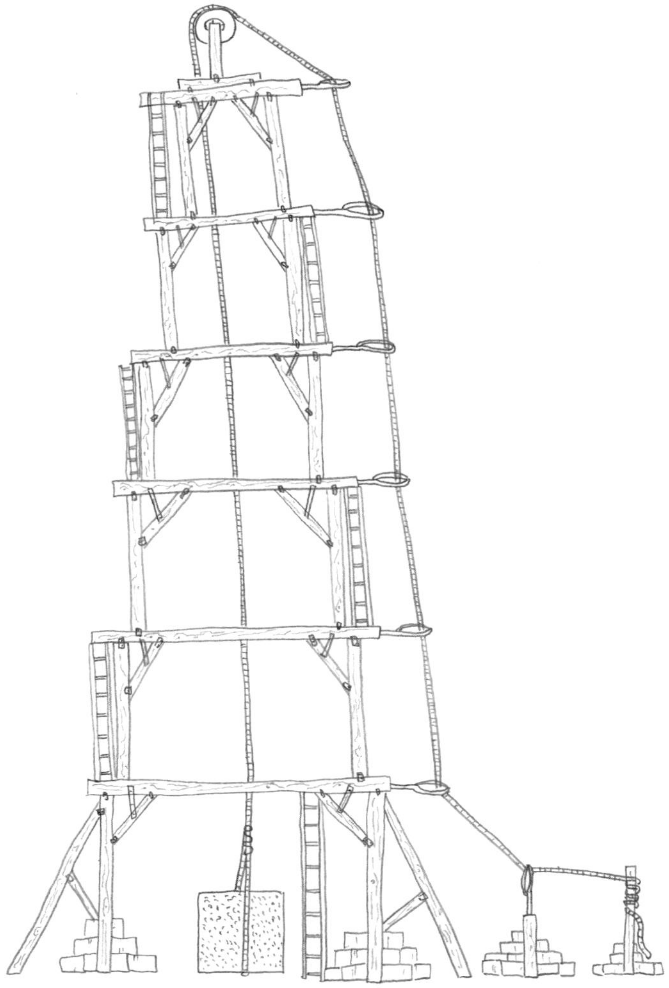

Tower
2005

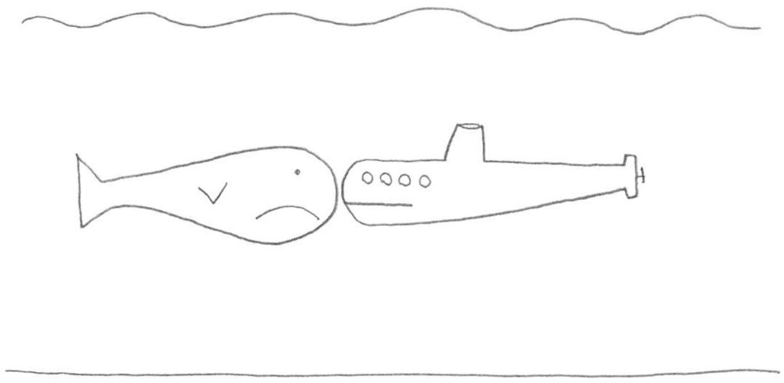

The Big Meeting
2007

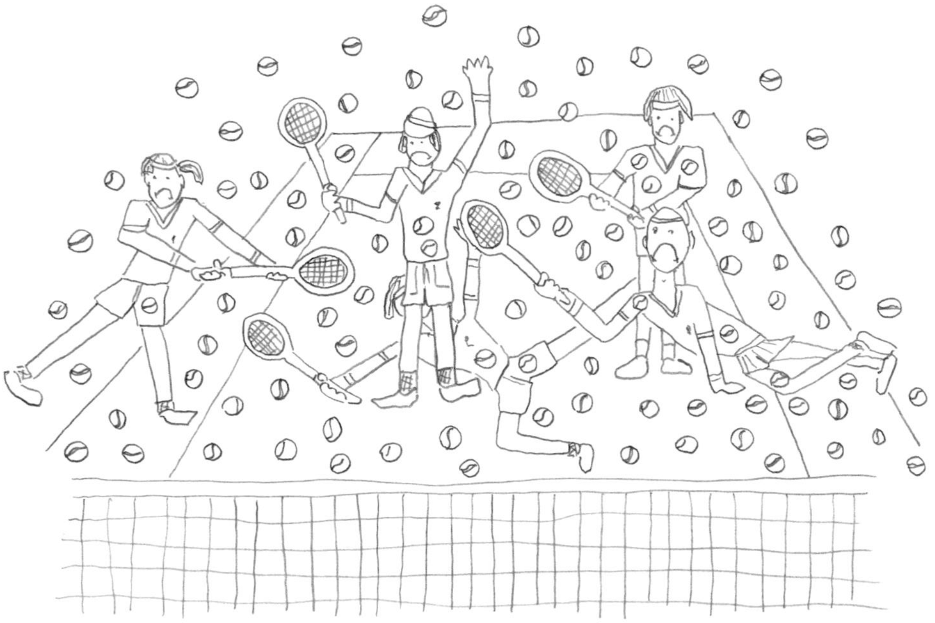

The Tennis Match
2005

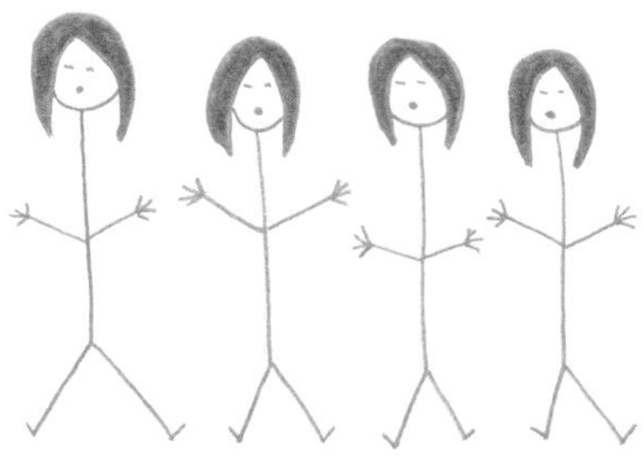

Tokyo Girls from Korea
2011

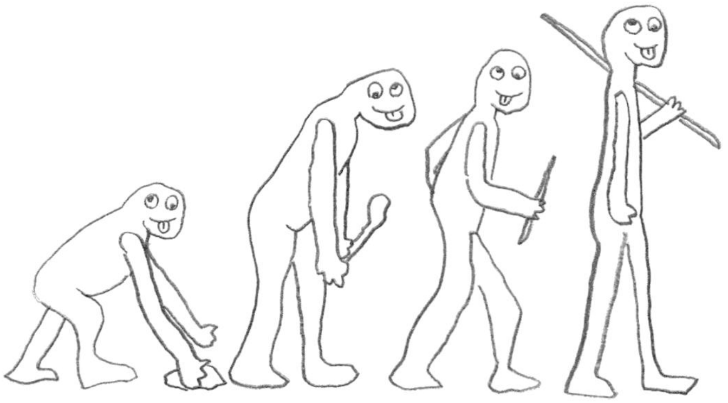

Always the Same Stupid Face
2007

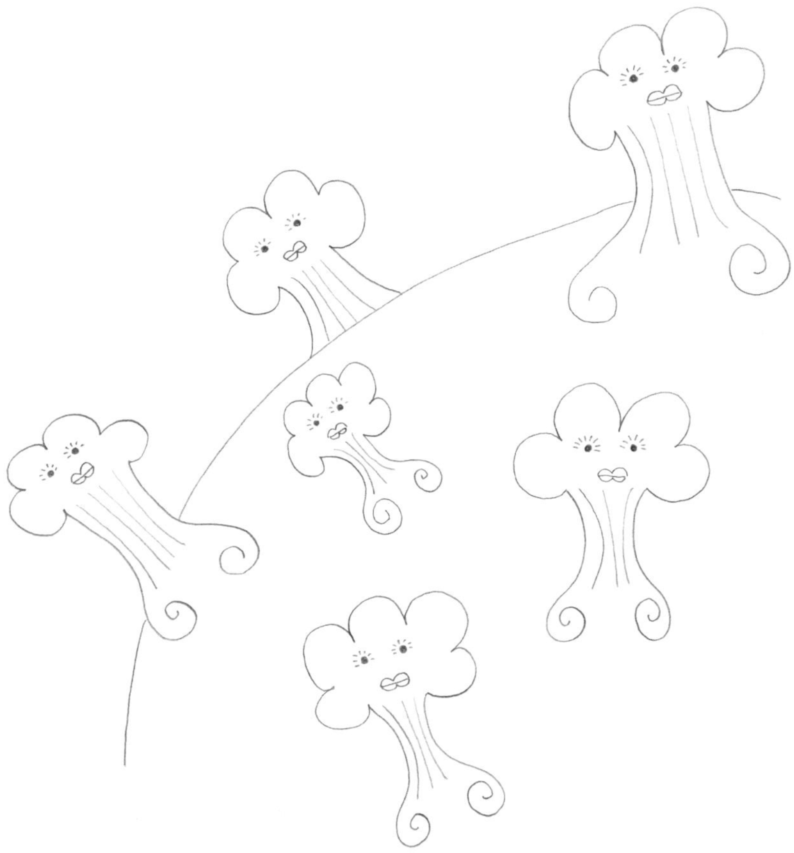

A-Bombs
2005

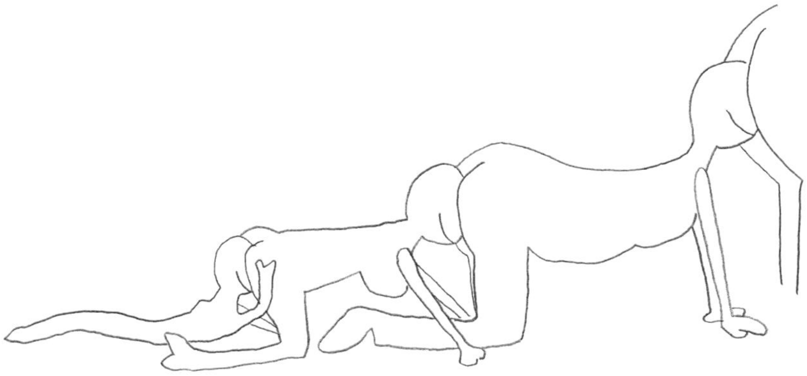

Ass After Ass
2010

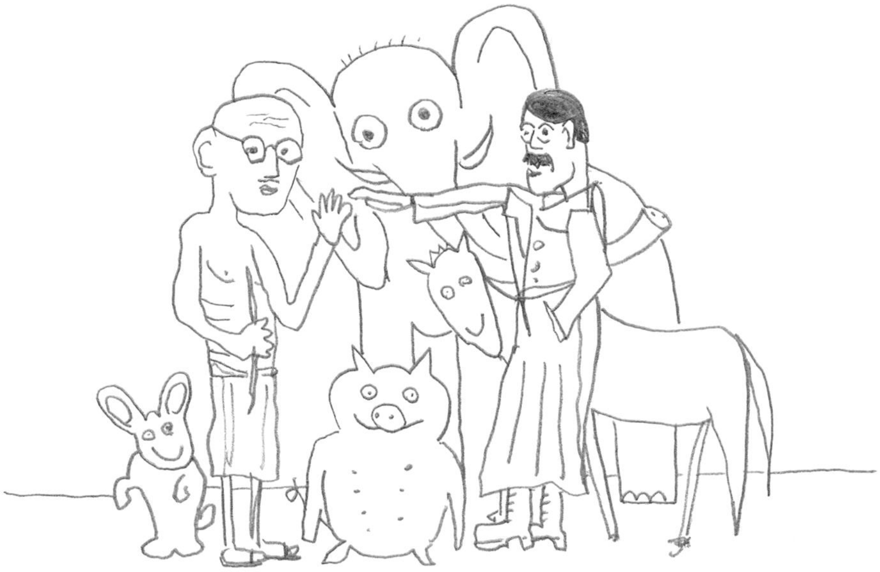

Animals Don't Understand
2009

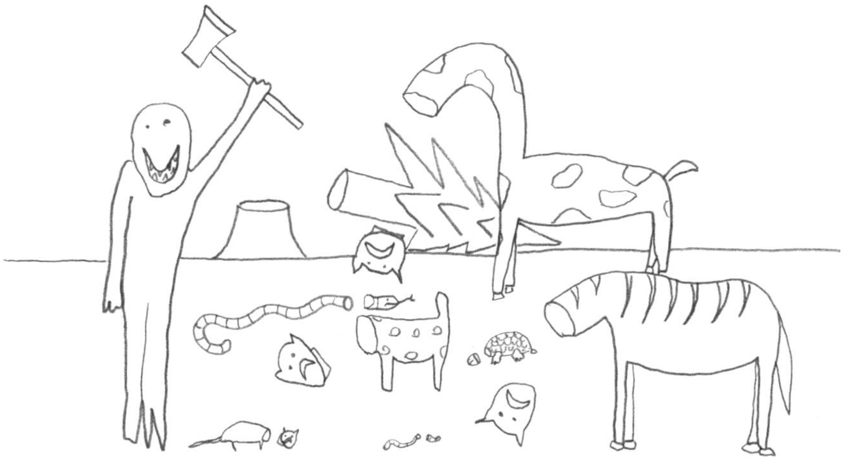

Brutalo
2014

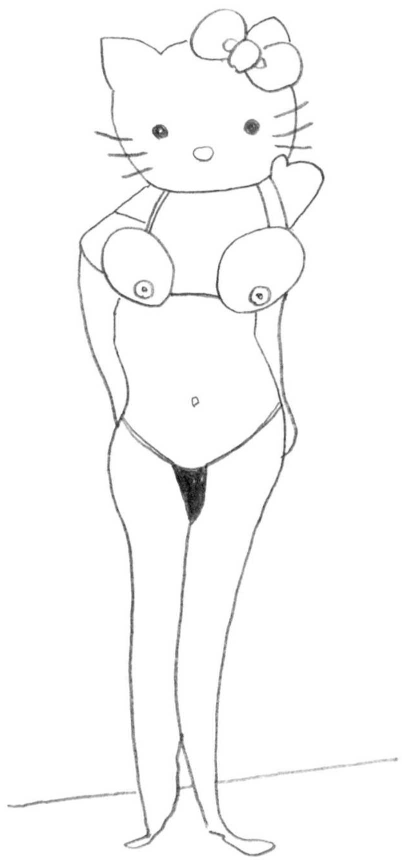

Sexy Kitty
2007

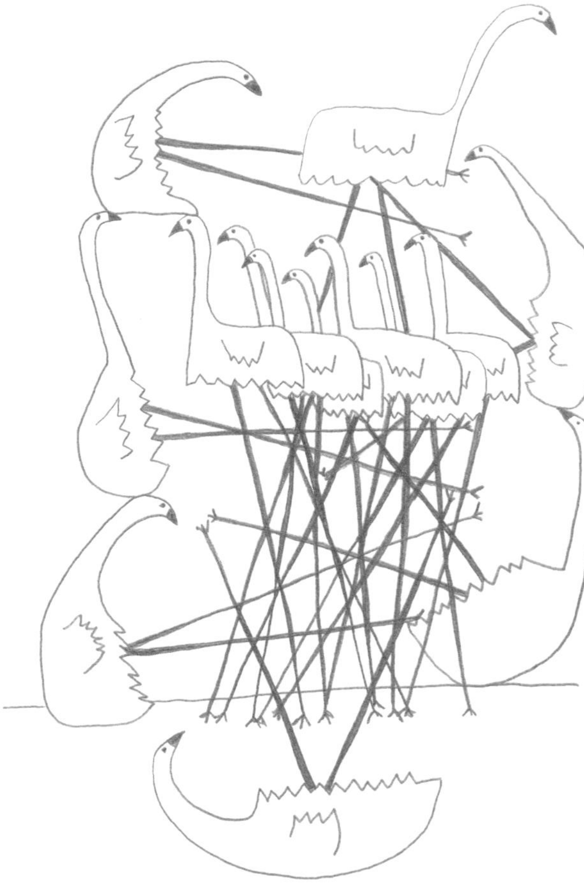

Nature Is Just Strange
2013

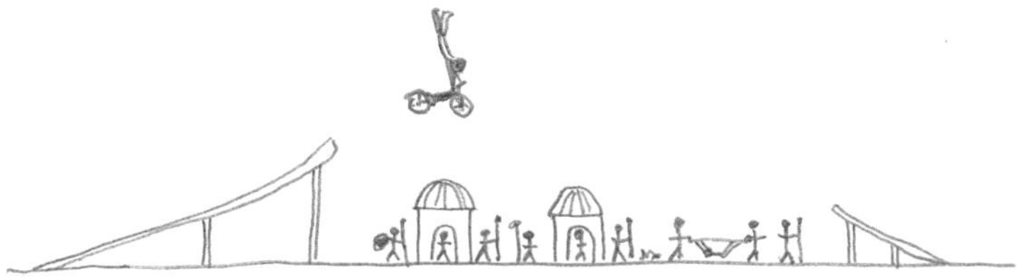

Big Jump
2007

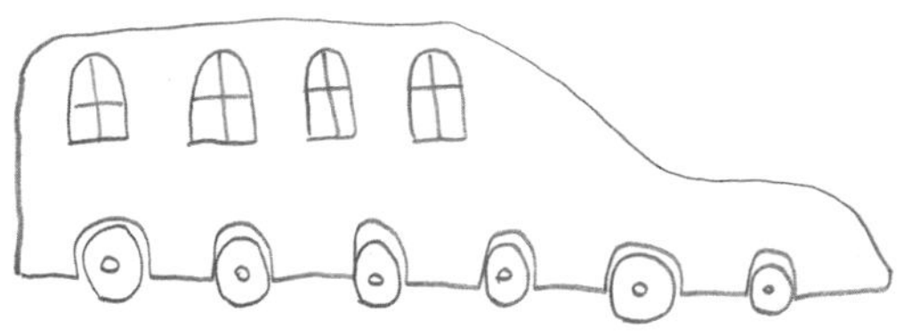

Car
2005

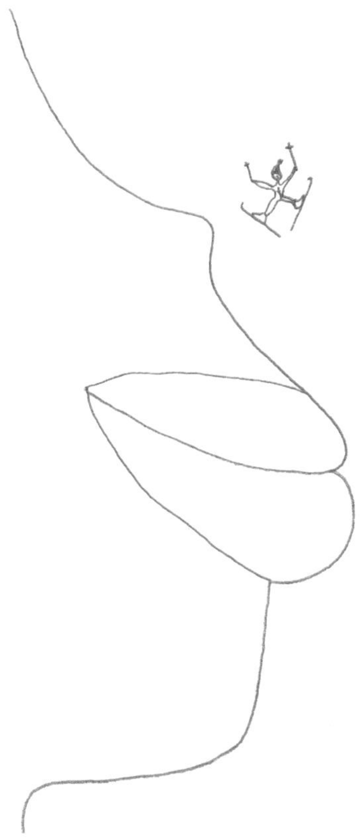

Die grosse Schanze
2015

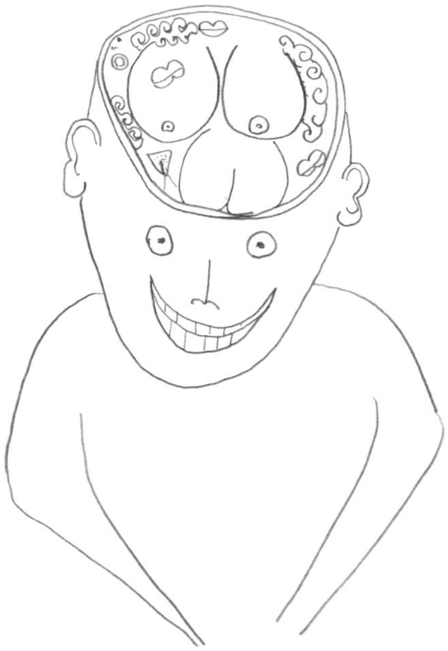

Dirty Mind
2005

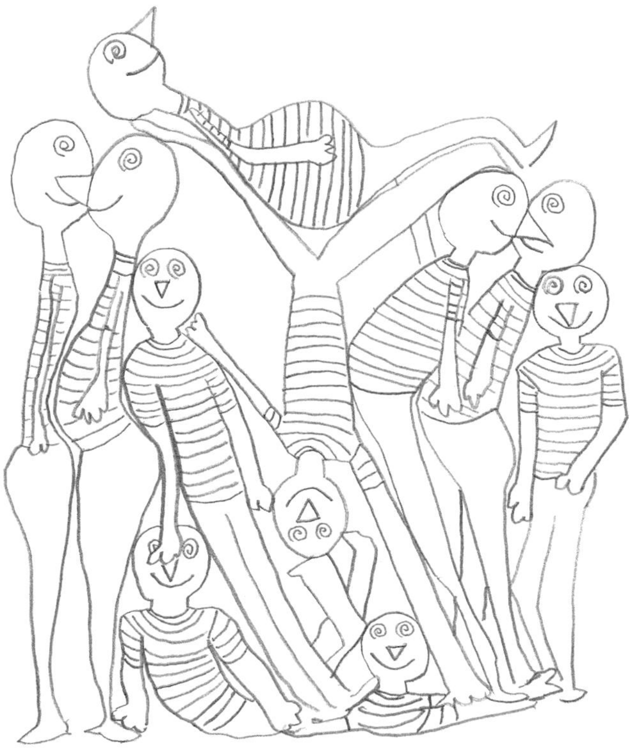

Funny Sailors
2012

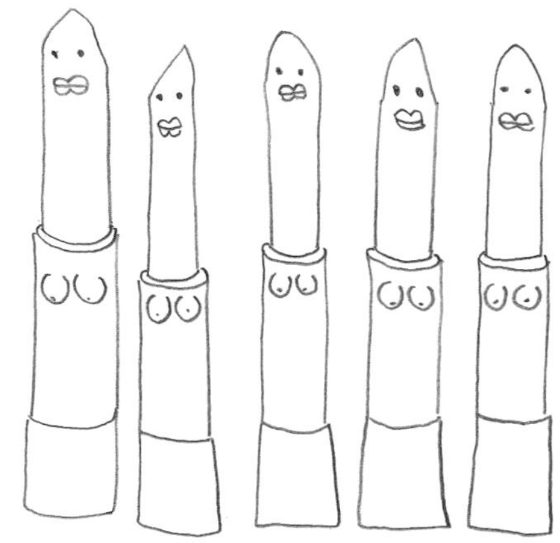

Girls Girls Girls
2005

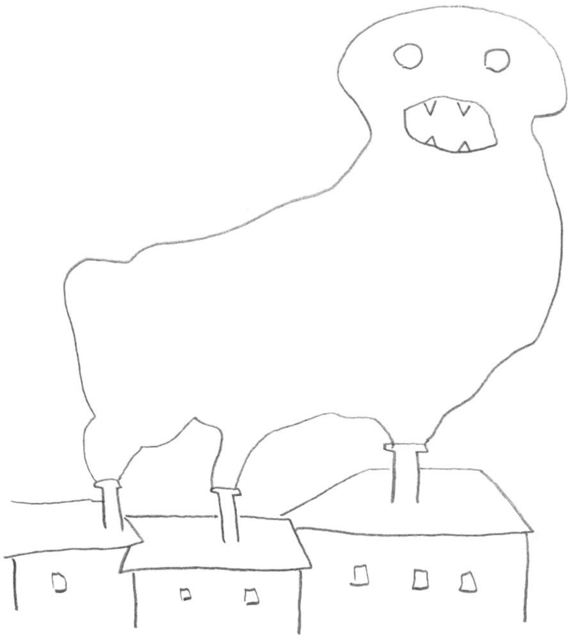

Global Warming
2008

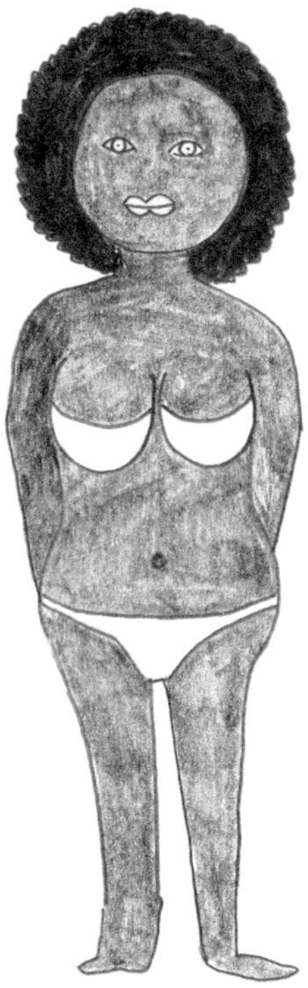

Foxy Brown
2010

No Obstacles to Drawing

Written by
Elsy Lahner

The way Olaf Breuning sees it, as an artist it is almost impossible to do anything these days that no one else has done before. Even in a globalized world, it is impracticable to be informed about everything, to know who is currently working on what and which artworks have just been made. It is therefore all the more important to Olaf Breuning to use his own unmistakable vocabulary in everything that he does.

Olaf Breuning works with what already exists, and produces references. Consequently, his works represent translations into his vocabulary or transformations into our time. For instance, in his Marilyn series of works (2010), Breuning referred to Andy Warhol's famous portraits of the film star, which today are among the icons of art history. For this appropriation, Olaf Breuning painted the faces of various women in vibrant colors and photographed them alone, in pairs, or in groups of four. It is fundamental, however, that he also showed the women's bodies, which, though they blend in with the photograph's background on account of being painted black, are clearly discernible as being naked. He thereby re-inserted a body into the portraits.

As in his other works—his films, photographs, and installations—Olaf Breuning also has recourse, in his drawing, to phenomena and media events that shape our collective experience. He showcases socially relevant themes and conflicts just as often as general knowledge from high culture and pop culture, even though these, in Olaf Breuning's opinion, are no longer valid categories and, certainly, pop art specifically has played its part in blurring the boundaries between the two.

Thus, he processes gender clichés (Oh, We Men Want It All so Much!, 2005), role models (Mother Nature, 2012), and religious stereotypes (Allah Is Big, 2005). He refers to Picasso's Guernica (There Is Always Someone Smiling, 2010) or Brueghel's Baummensch (Hironimus Hosch, 2008); in other drawings, by contrast, to the latest selfie by Kim Kardashian (Please Don't Watch, 2015), E.T. (I Hate Email, 2005), or to his observation of conversation among American girls, with their habit of constantly commentating their phrases with "Oh my God" (OMG, 2013).

Some drawings are based on personal experiences, and therefore can be understood only by the initiated few; others, due to their currentness, are presumably comprehensible solely in the here and now. The drawing Idiots, for example, which was created in 2007 and shows people standing in a row, each engrossed in their own respective mobile phone calls, might already look entirely different today, around 10 years later. Presumably, each of these same people would now be staring at the smartphones in their hands and occasionally swiping a finger across the screen. Olaf Breuning's drawings therefore also become chronological documents, a mirror of our time.

Humor, too, is often comprehensible only in the context of the respective era—in multiple cases, in a certain culture only—and, also, what is regarded as funny at one time depends strongly upon present-day moral notions. For example, the oafish clown slipping on a banana skin, or the custard pie so widespread in slapstick, is found to be less funny these days than it used to be. Yet precisely because of this temporal reference, humor, and hence humorous art as well, fulfills an essential task.

In addition to its role as an outlet, humor is able to react critically to everyday conflicts and societal themes without pointing the moral finger.

Black humor, specifically, often ranges beyond the boundaries of the politically correct, and sparks controversies precisely in that way. To what violent and over-the-top reactions even simple cartoons can lead when they depict certain circumstances in a forthright manner was demonstrated, not least, by the attack on the editorial team of satirical magazine Charlie Hebdo in 2015.

To Olaf Breuning, humor is an essential instrument, an important aspect of his vocabulary with which he, with plenty of self-irony and as part of the society that he describes, reproduces his observations.

His drawings are pointed comments on our everyday life or on up-to-the-minute events.

Occasionally ironic, sharp-tongued, or cynical, sometimes absurd and sometimes refreshingly banal. In their humor, but in their simplicity, too, they are not dissimilar to those of David Shrigley or even Dan Perjovschi. Shrigley and Perjovschi likewise work in a very reduced manner, monochromatically, and combine their drawings from time to time with text; nevertheless, all three artists have their own distinct style, their own signature, and the concern behind each is a different one.

What is further common to them, however, is the characteristic that their drawings are deliberately to be found outside the art context, too—in the case of Breuning and Shrigley, on T-shirts, textile bags, and similar; with regard to Dan Perjovschi, on house walls and newspaper pages. The aim of all three is to use their statements to reach an audience beyond the vernissages, with no great inhibitions.

Olaf Breuning calls it: "Art for everyone." Art without limits. But he is not concerned about pandering to mass taste or how much his art is liked. His chief concern is to have his works, which are produced in our time, refer directly to this time as well and, in this way, constantly challenge him to new things.

Perhaps for this reason, too, Olaf Breuning's drawings are not made in the seclusion of his studio, but in the midst of events, in cafés, in restaurants, in waiting rooms. If Olaf Breuning were living in Vienna, he would probably connect with the long tradition of artists who work in Vienna coffeehouses, and observe and draw for hours on end.

It appears as though Olaf Breuning, contrary to planning his works in the studio, immerses himself entirely in the things going on around him and, even more than usually, works from his gut and proceeds largely intuitively—like a seismographer who detects movements and charts them straight away.

He produces the drawings in small A6 Muji sketchbooks and in pencil, so that he can perform swift changes with the eraser. Only certain works are selected by the artist later on, and realized once again in the larger US Letter Size format (21.59 × 27.94 cm), literally "drawn in." Only his selected works receive titles, which describe his drawings only briefly or add a reference as well. Olaf Breuning therefore works spontaneously and in a planned manner all at the same time.

This applies also to his solo exhibition Small Brain, Big Stomach in 2009, at his Metro Pictures gallery in New York. For this presentation, Olaf Breuning translated some of his drawings into a large format for the first time, working with thick black strokes directly on the wall. These wall-works were supplemented by objects in wood and black acrylic, which likewise were based on his drawings and were thus transformed into three-dimensional drawings in space.

The fact that the traditional drawing on paper manages without particular technical aids—apart from a simple pencil—and can be made swiftly anywhere, ad-hoc, is a particularity of drawing that certainly suits Olaf Breuning very well. In addition, the drawing and the act of drawing is familiar to all of us, from our first childhood drawing to absent-minded doodling during a telephone call—various factors that contribute to an understanding of his drawings and correspond to Olaf Breuning's concept of "art for everyone."

His drawings look straightforward, and convey an ease that encourages people to confront and analyze them. Despite this ostensible ease, however, a profound seriousness is concealed behind them.

In addition to the USA and Europe, in other words: western culture, from which he draws his main references, the artist and his works are also popular in Japan in particular. A contributing role in this is played by the fact that many phenomena described by Olaf Breuning arise in this cultural sphere as well. However, his visual vocabulary doubtlessly also plays a big part in this popularity. For example, faces are of crucial significance and are constant companions in Olaf Breuning's works. (Even the drawn hand on the cover of this publication bears one!) This is also the case in Japan. Faces can be found here on practically every poster and every piece of packaging. Conversely, Olaf Breuning has recourse to Japanese visual vocabulary, too—emojis, to which he makes reference in his eponymous photographic works from 2014, are a Japanese invention (e: picture; moji: character).

Cartoon and comic also have a long tradition precisely in Japan. Manga, freely translated as "uncontrolled image" (man: spontaneous, impulsive, random, uninhibited; ga: image), is omnipresent as a narrative form there and is received in all population groups.

For Olaf Breuning's drawings can absolutely be described as cartoons.

First, in accordance with today's customary meaning, and second, in the original sense, too. For, in the Middle Ages, "cartoons," derived from the French "carton," designated the sketches for frescoes or tapestries, the preliminary drawings on cardboard for an artwork. Most of Olaf Breuning's first drawings took the form of painstaking sketches for his elaborate photographic enactments. By contrast, his present-day drawings correspond to the classic cartoons that might be printed in newspapers and magazines.

With his drawing style, Olaf Breuning connects with those artists who, in the 1980s and 1990s, arrived at a new narrative form in drawing by taking inspiration from the most diverse fields of graphic art and combining them in their works. Style elements of 19th-century drawing, such as that of Francisco de Goya, for example, or Odilon Redon or even the caricatures of Honoré Daumier, were used along with folk art or children's book illustrations. The artists did not even balk at allowing influences from sub-cultures of visual art or music, too, such as the punk scene, for instance. Thus, comic and cartoon also found their way into drawing, and indeed not—as previously in pop art with Andy Warhol or Roy Lichtenstein—as conceptual appropriations, but as real stylistic means. Despite their different origins, artists such as Raymond Pettibon, Pavel Pepperstein, or Yoshitomo Nara began making use of this practice in parallel to one another and, in doing so, referred —or refer still—to their respective geographic life-center and their own socio-cultural background.

Katharine Stout writes, aptly: "The amateurish-looking works of these artists, low-tech, cheap and quick to produce, easy to distribute and seen as unpretentious, appealed immediately to audiences who were also listening to pop and dance music, produced in their bedrooms on new affordable recording software." And: "The instant visual appeal of these drawing styles, often annotated with everyday language, which emerged from surprisingly numerous artists across different parts of the world at this time, might appear at first glance to be due to its naïvety and playfulness. Yet more often than not, this is a stealth tactic that allows a biting and insightful social critique."

Much of this is true of Olaf Breuning's works as well. The latter goes one step further with his drawings, however; he dispenses with all other forms of stylistic borrowing and restricts himself with absolute rigor exclusively to cartoon elements.

In addition, in contrast to the above-named artists, drawing, to him, is not the primary or exclusive means of expression. His drawings can therefore be seen in the context of his other works. For his themes, humor, and visual vocabulary are the same here as well—just re-interpreted for drawing.

Precisely because of this, though, it is delightful to consider the drawings separately and autonomously—and to think about what Olaf Breuning intends with them. Do his drawings function, in his view, as extracts, in a way, or—if you like—as a parallel rail, which he can use to react to current phenomena or events simply more quickly and directly? Or is he using them to range deliberately in an artistic gray area, on the boundary toward applied art, maybe the mass medium, similarly to the way in which he also often exaggerates his photographic works in the direction of kitsch?

For, not least, Olaf Breuning is concerned with one more thing: questioning what constitutes visual art today. With the blurring lines of separation, toward other fields. With the criteria that establish when something is ascribable to high culture and when it is to be described as a consumer item.

And, sometimes, both are apt: the glass is half empty and half full at the same time.

Sources:

Interview with Olaf Breuning on September 12th, 2016

Laura Hoptman, Drawing Now. Eight Propositions. The Museum of Modern Art, New York 2002

Katharine Stout, Contemporary Drawing from the 1960s to Now. Tate Publishing 2014

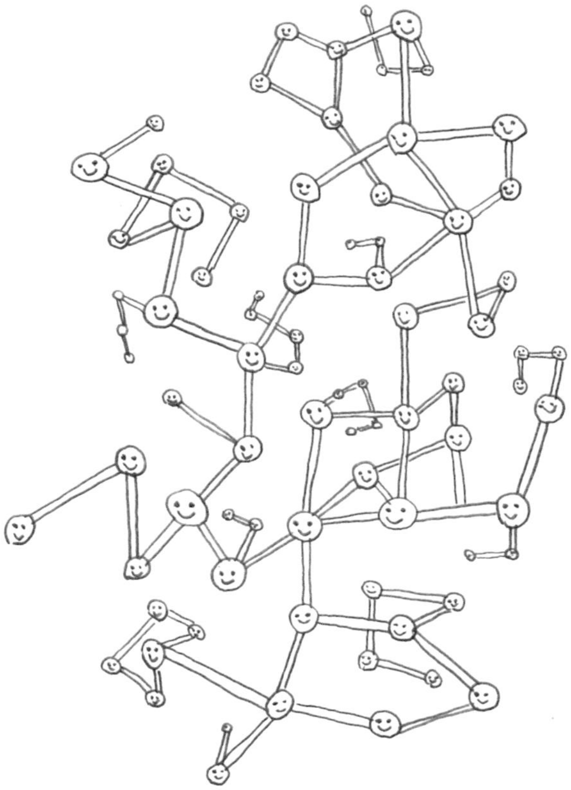

Good Genes
2008

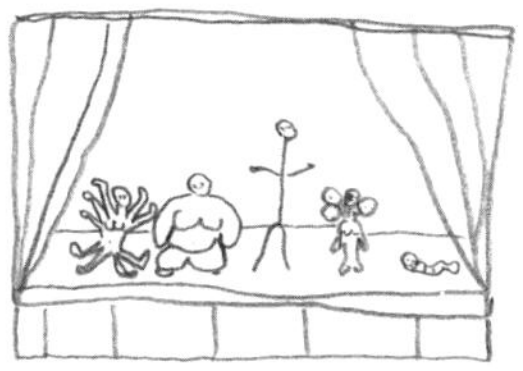

Freakshow
2009

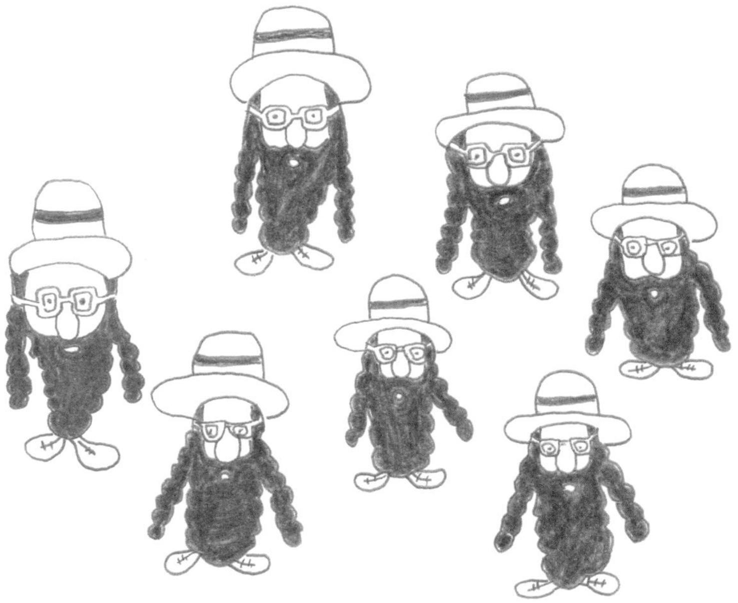

Jews
2015

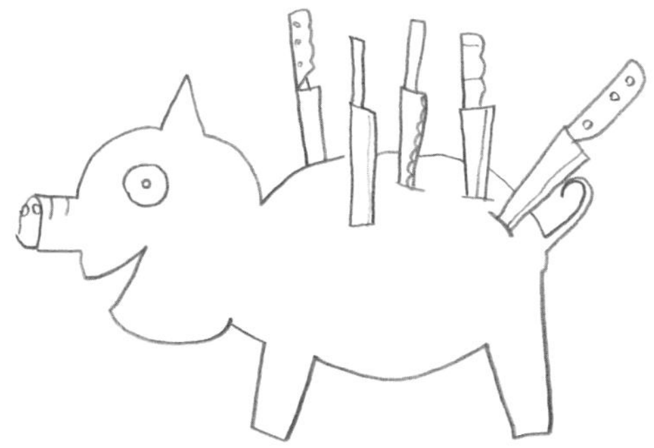

Happy Pig
2005

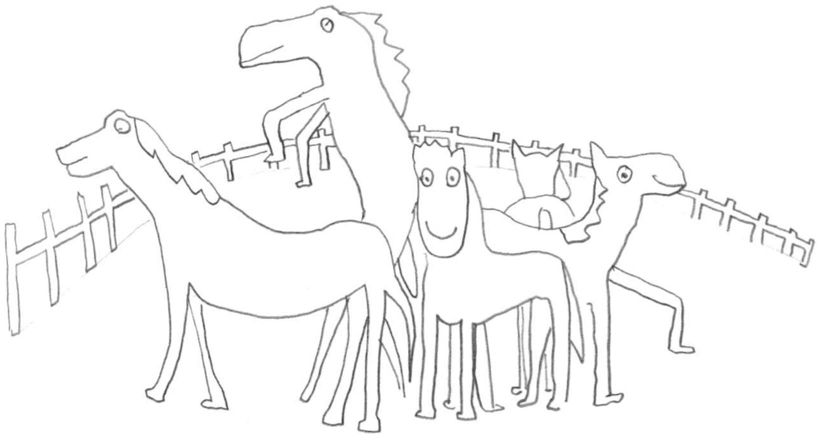

Horses Are Funny Creatures
2005

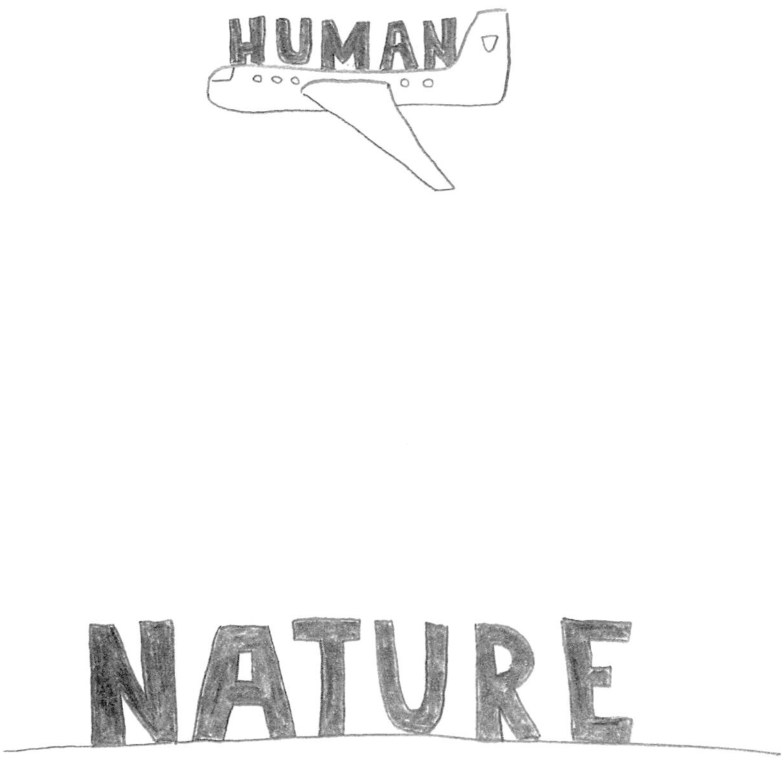

Human Nature
2010

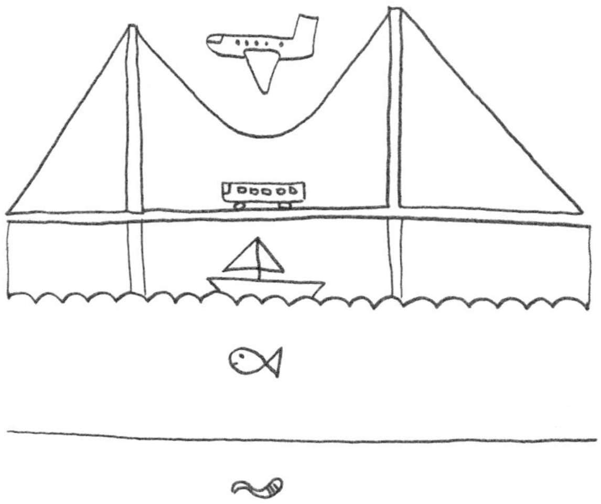

What a Coincidence
2011

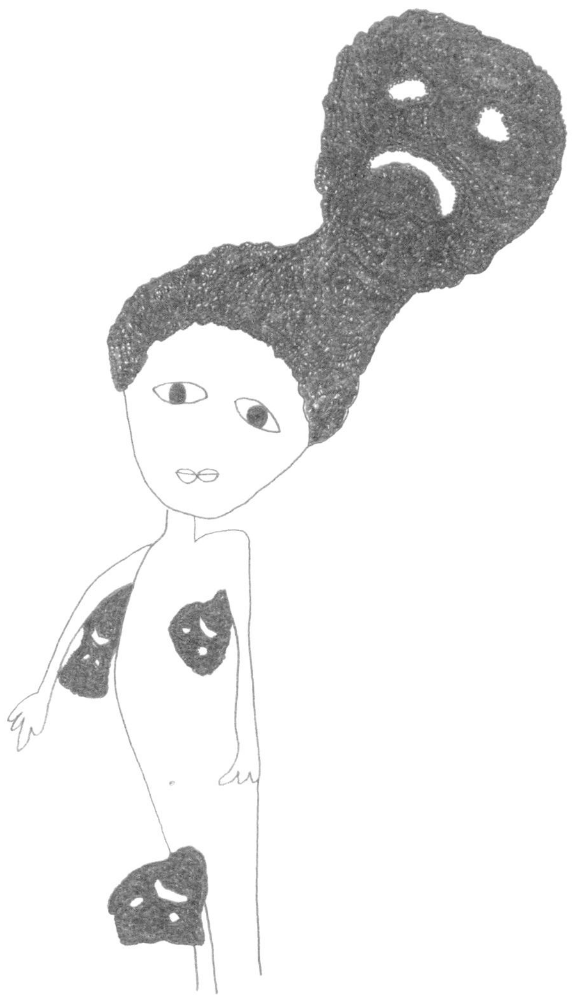

Italian Woman
2015

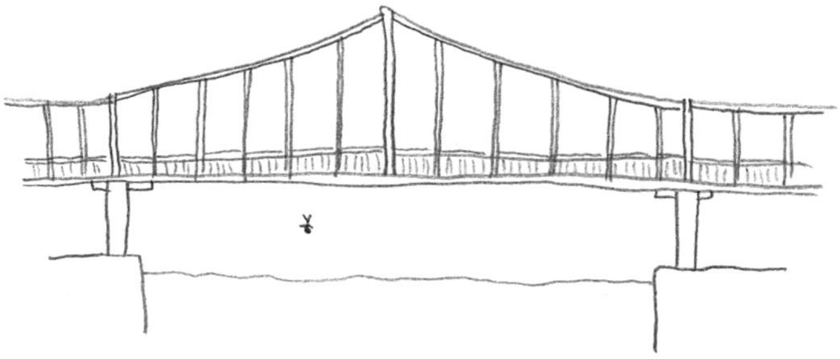

Last Day
2009

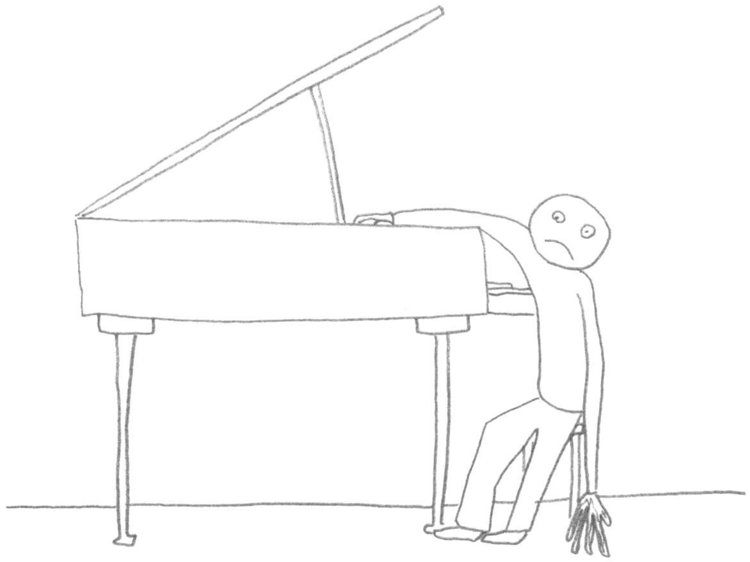

Just Tired
2015

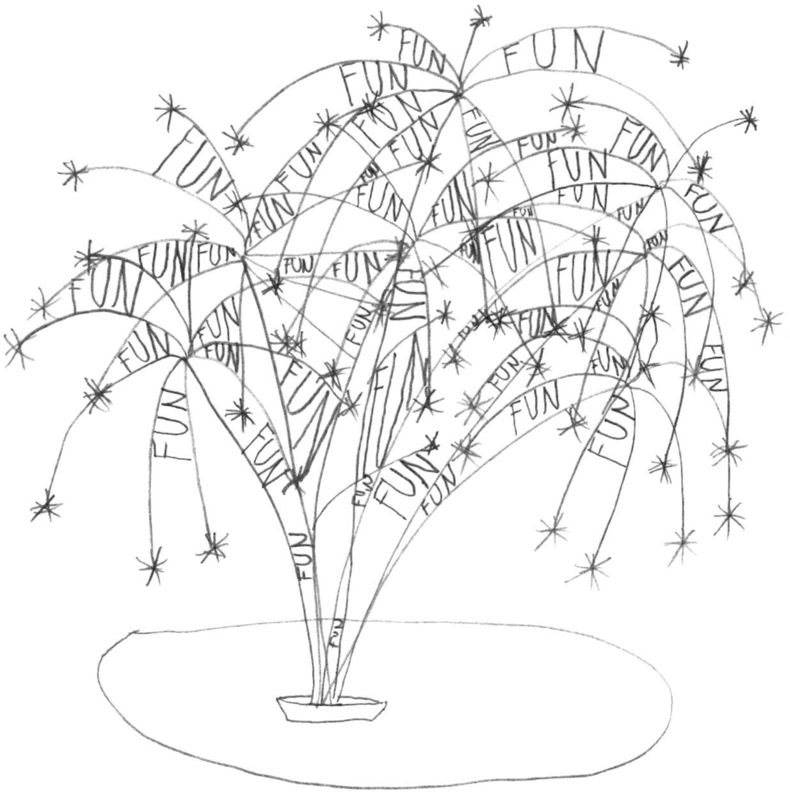

More Fun
2008

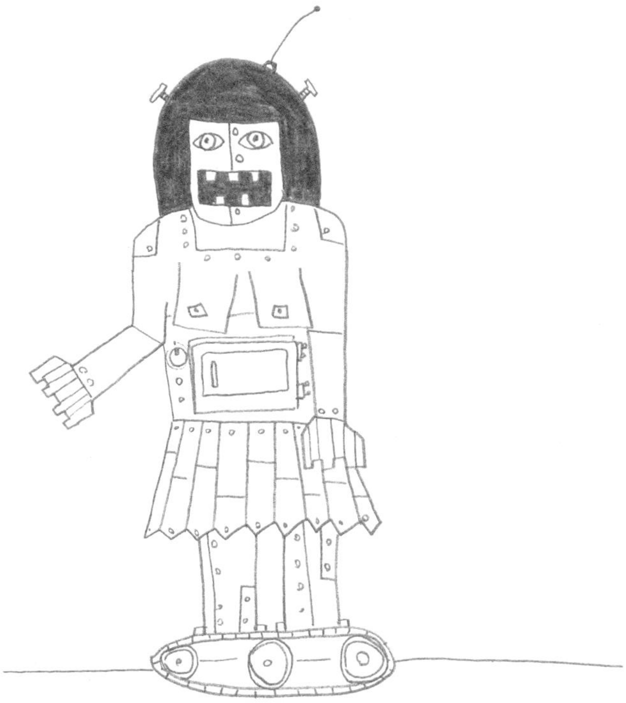

Japanese Robot
2012

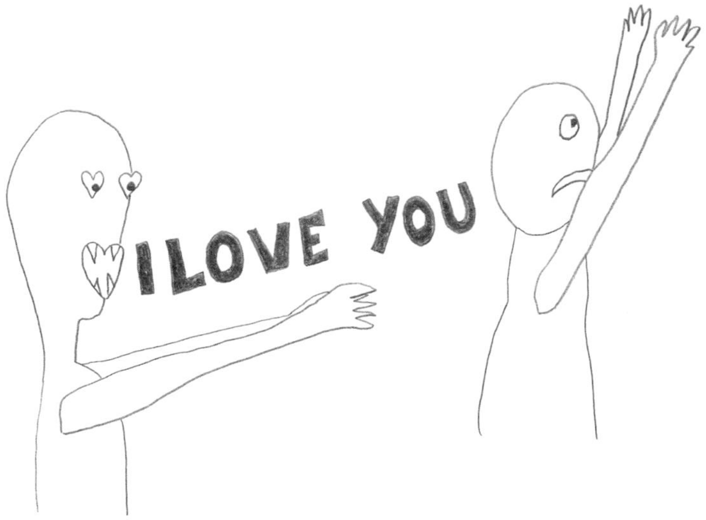

I Love You
2007

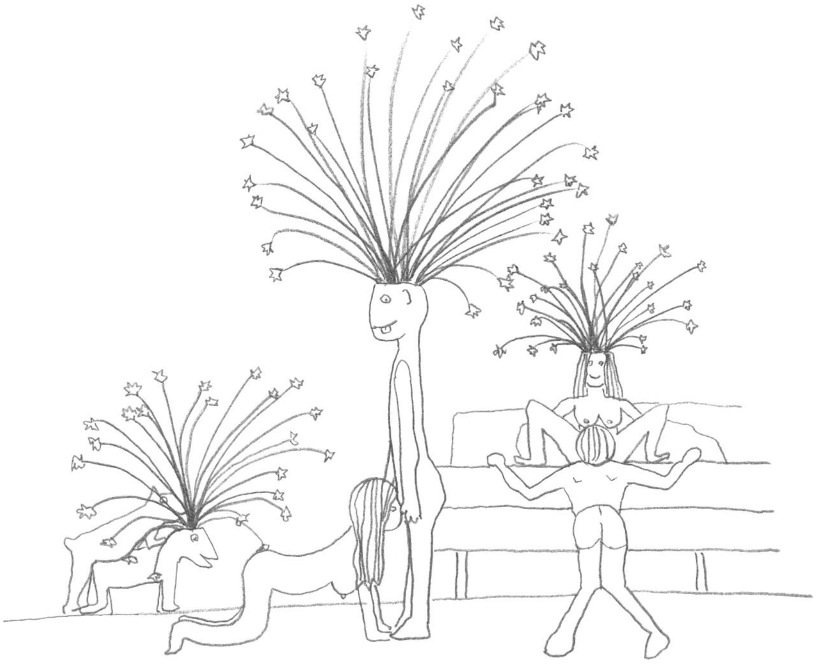

Oh Yes
2007

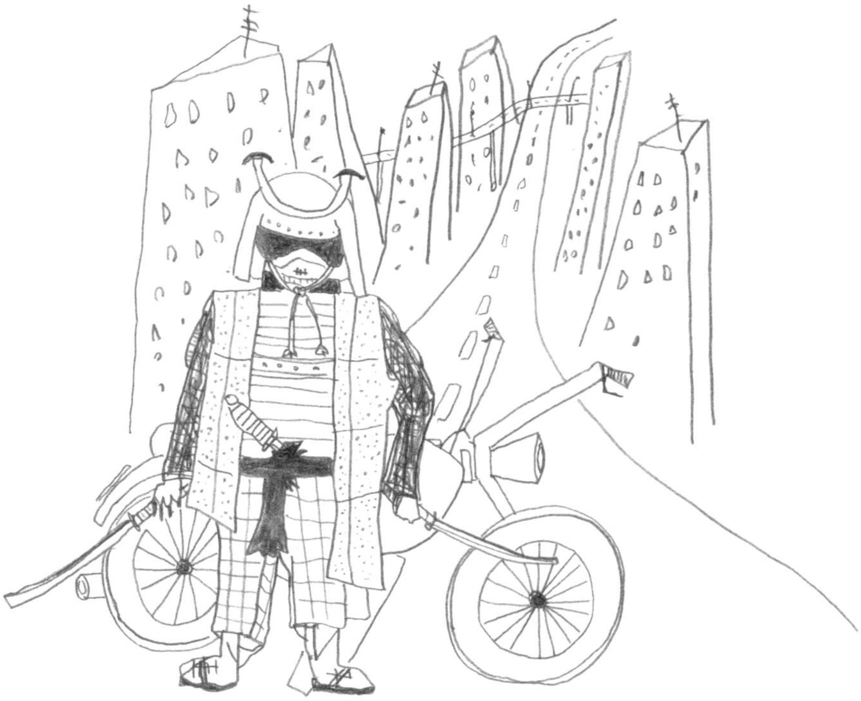

Last Samurai
2011

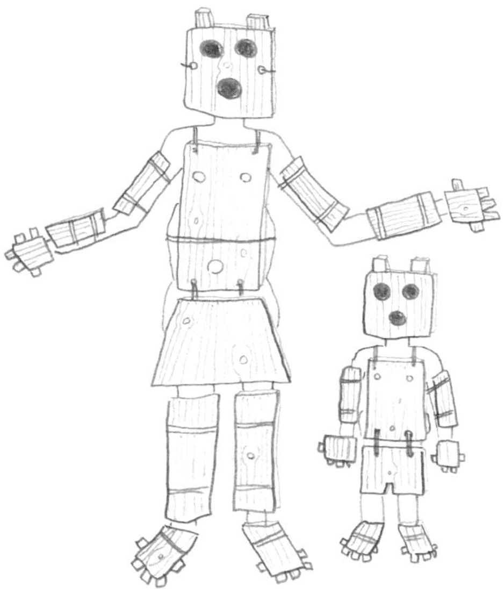

Mother and Child
2005

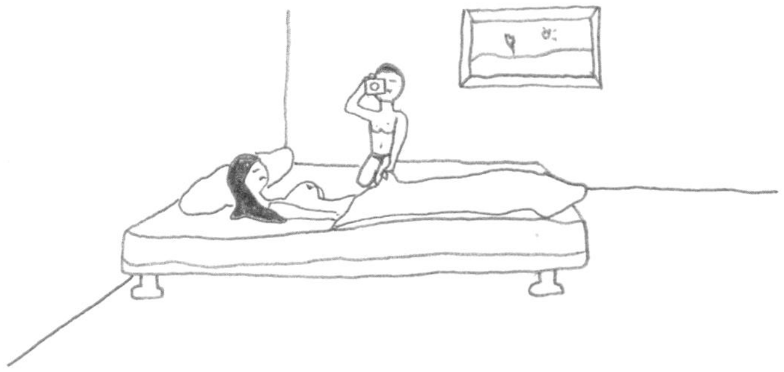

The Man and the Indian Girl
2011

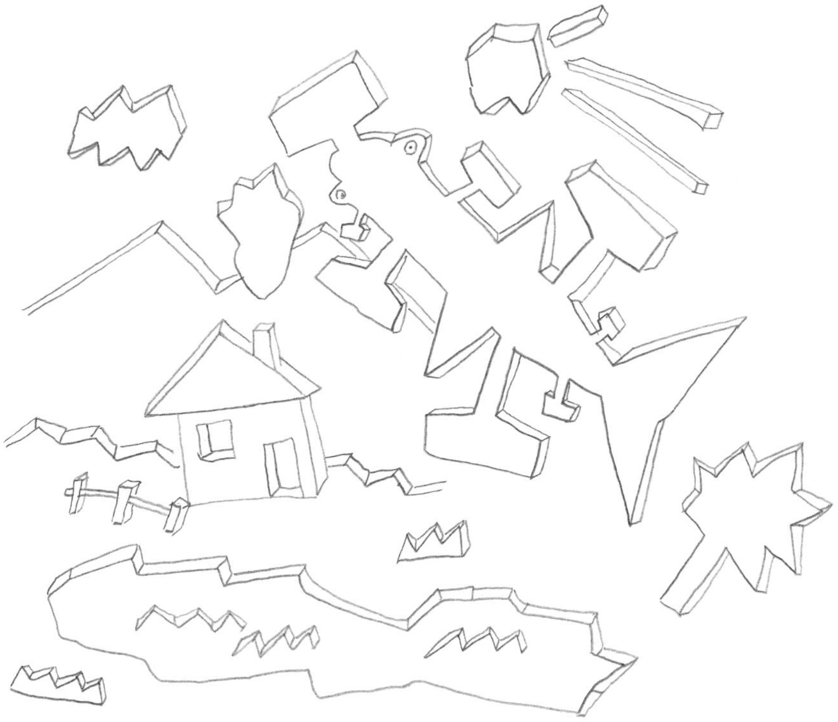

The Hammer Fish
2005

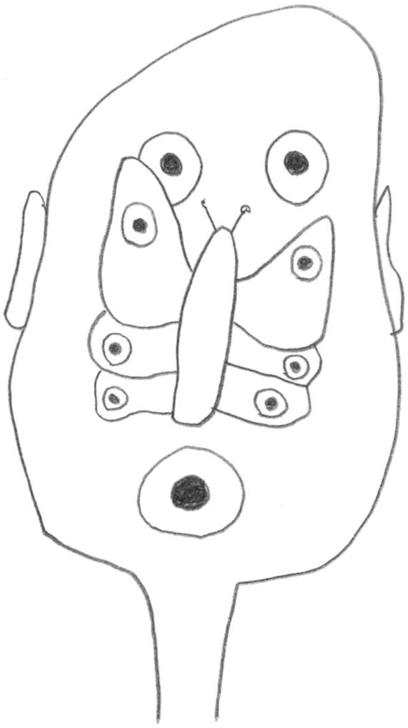

Hide Butterfly Hide
2007

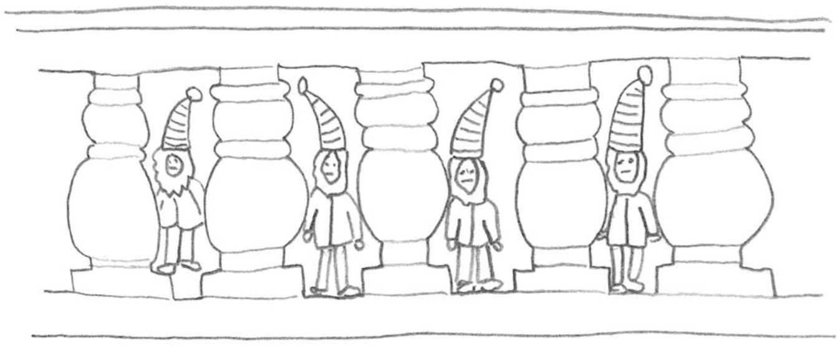

Too Small to Be True
2005

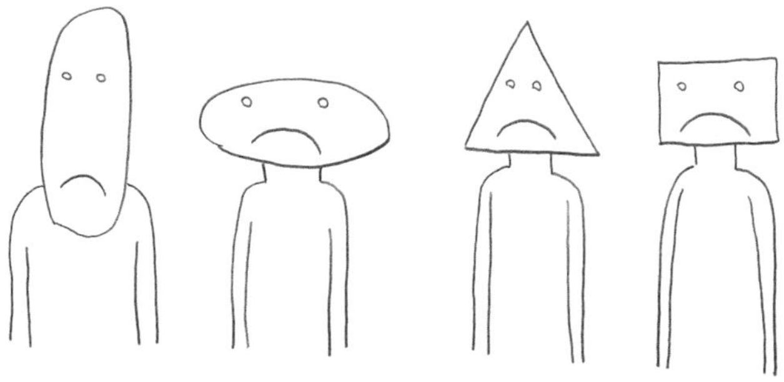

Thinkers
2007

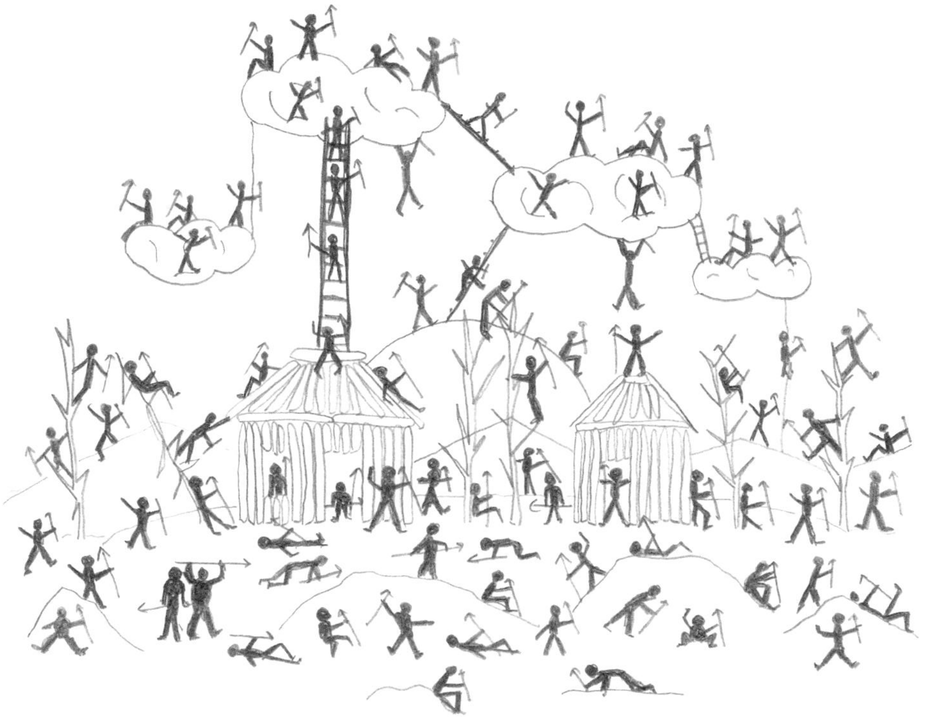

Why Should We Relax?
2005

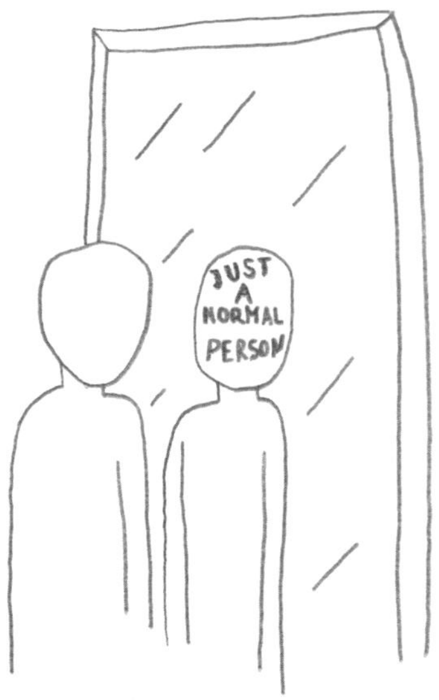

Just a Normal Person
2011

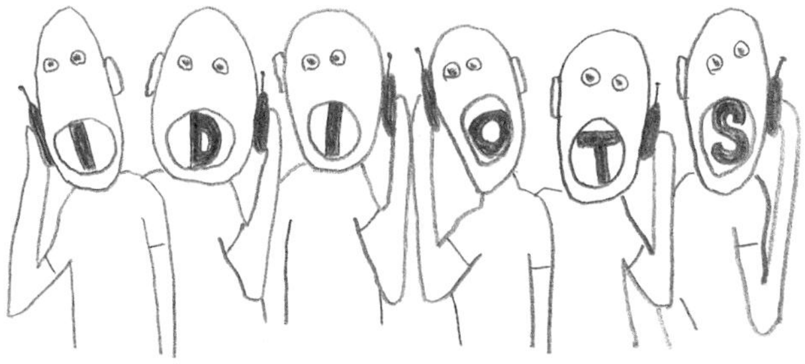

Idiots
2007

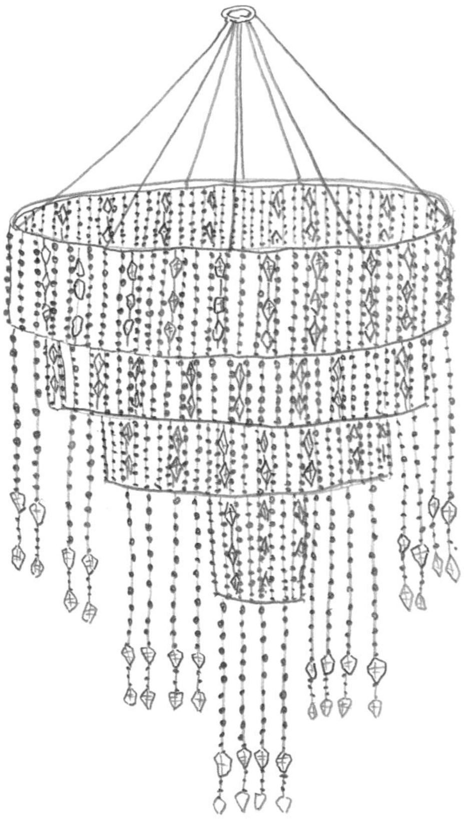

Kronleuchter
2005

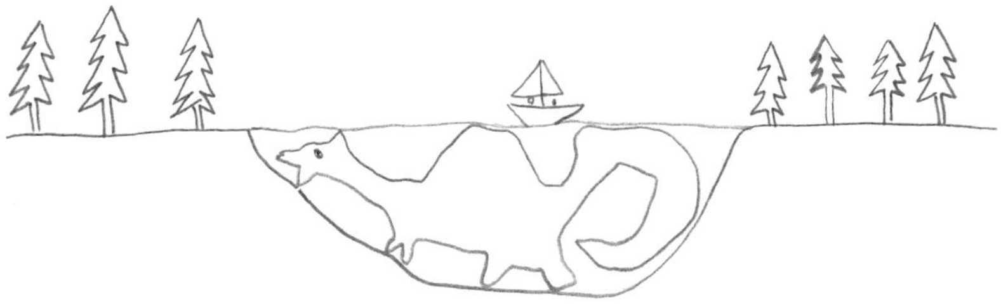

Loch Ness
2007

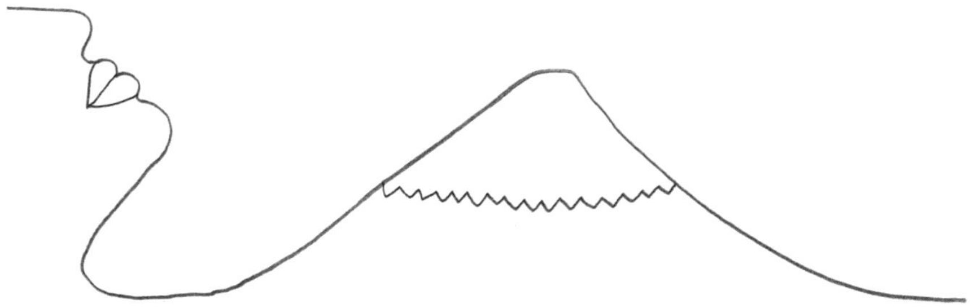

Mount Fuji
2007

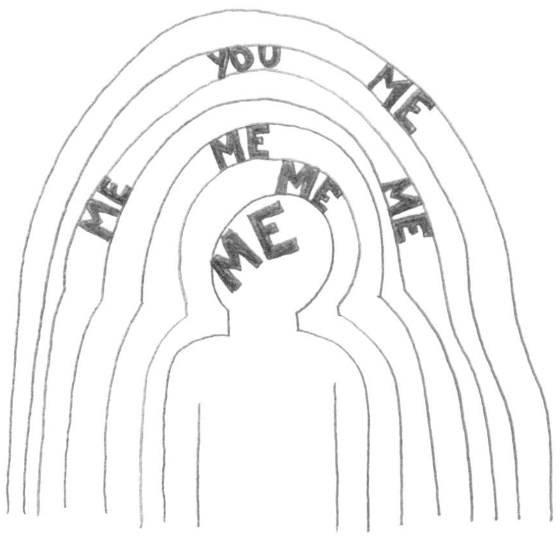

Me Me Me You Me Me
2007

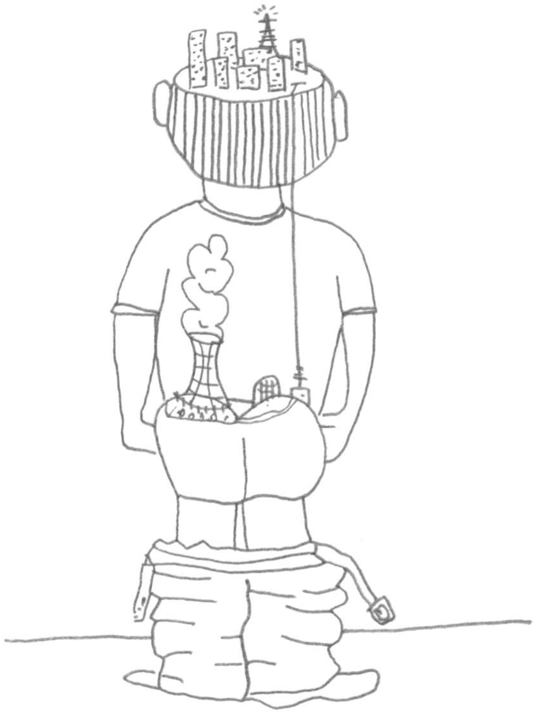

Mister Generator
2012

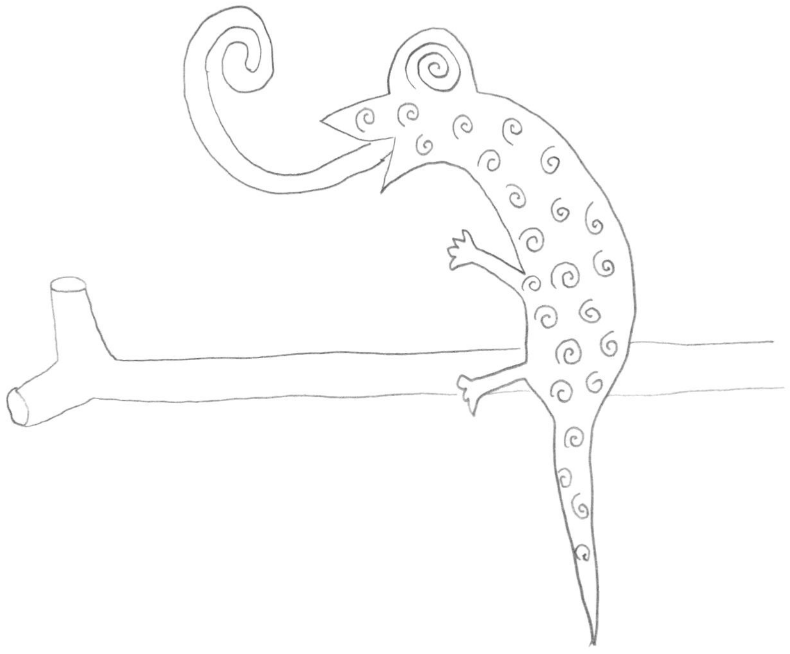

I Am What I See
2005

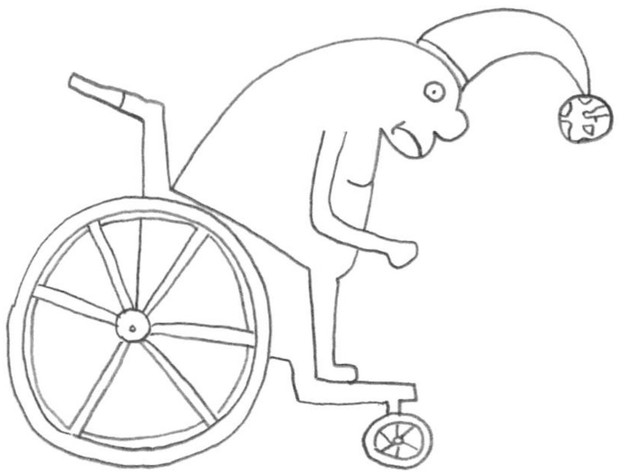

Alter Pessimist
2005

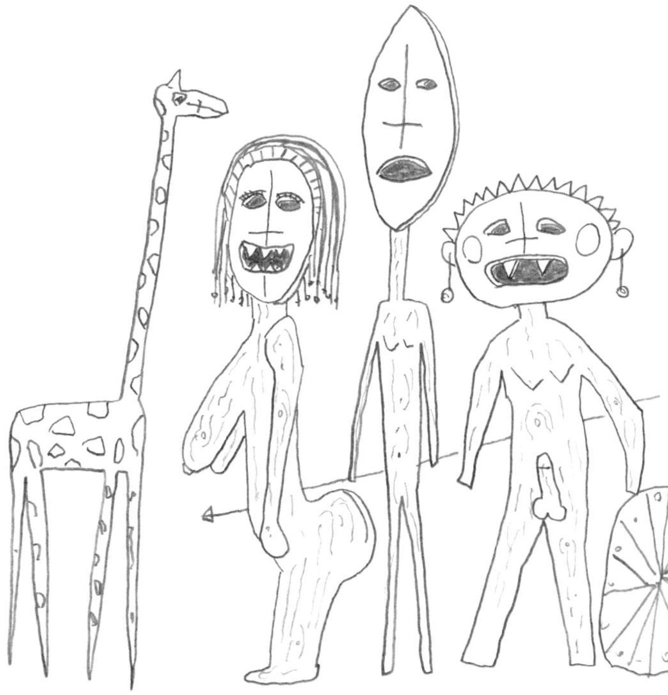

Africans
2005

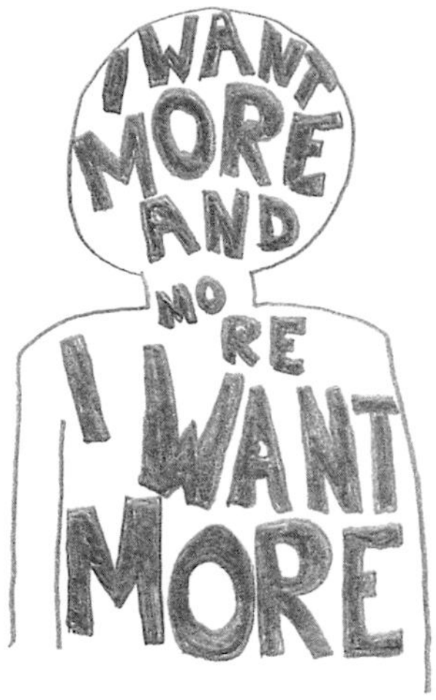

I Want More
2007

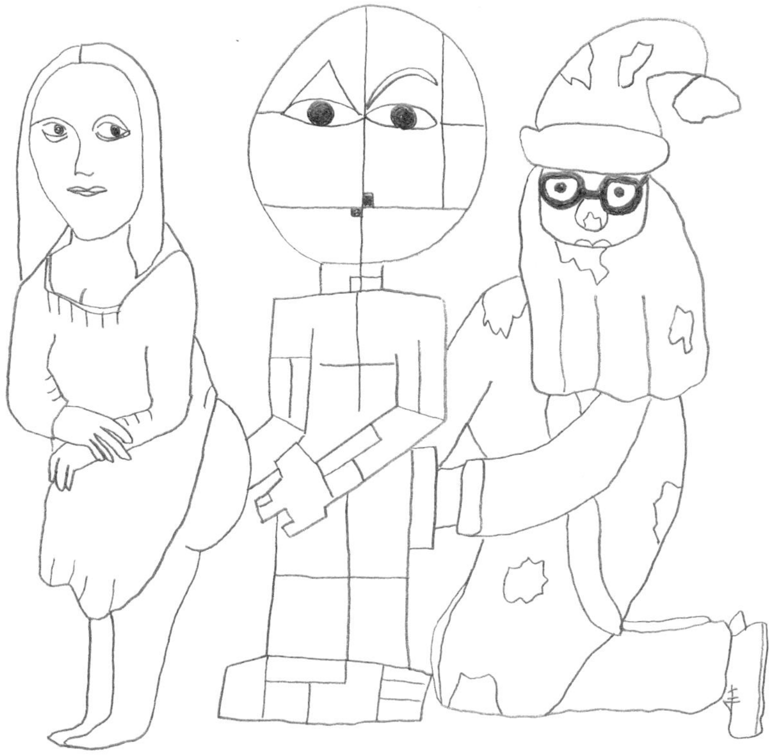

Art History Fucks Itself
2007

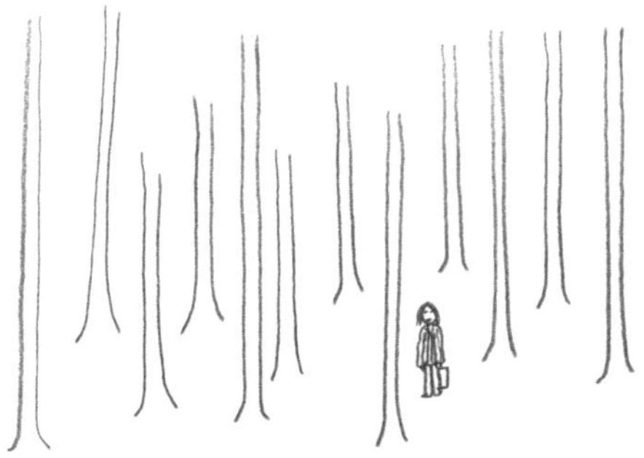

I Am so Lonely
2016

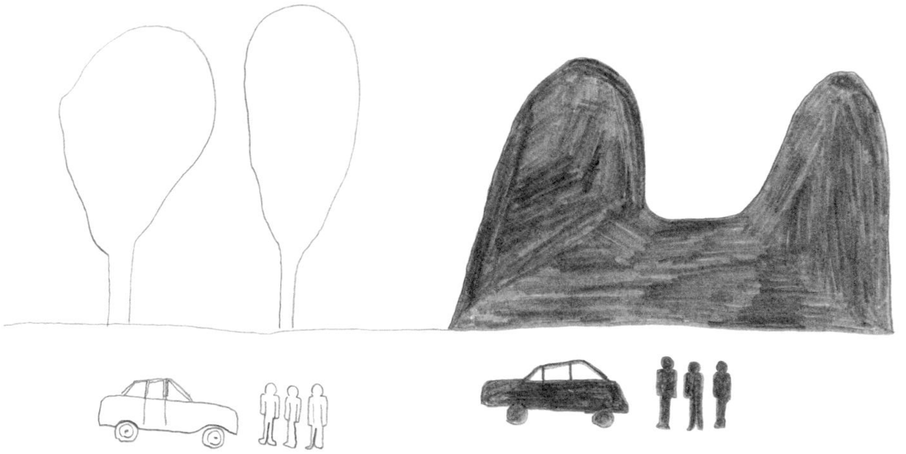

Black and White
2005

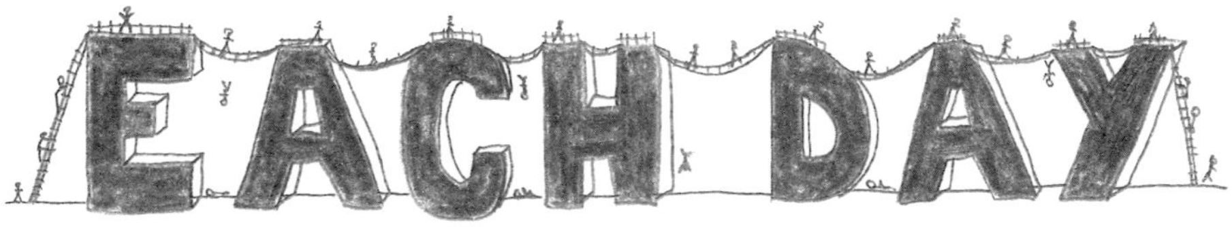

Each Day
2010

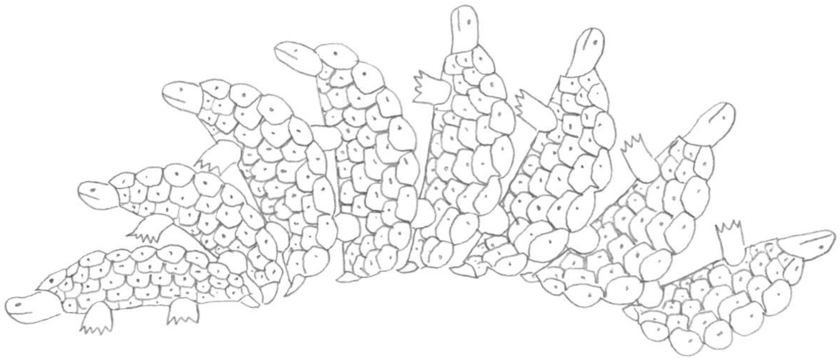

Stupid Turtles
2005

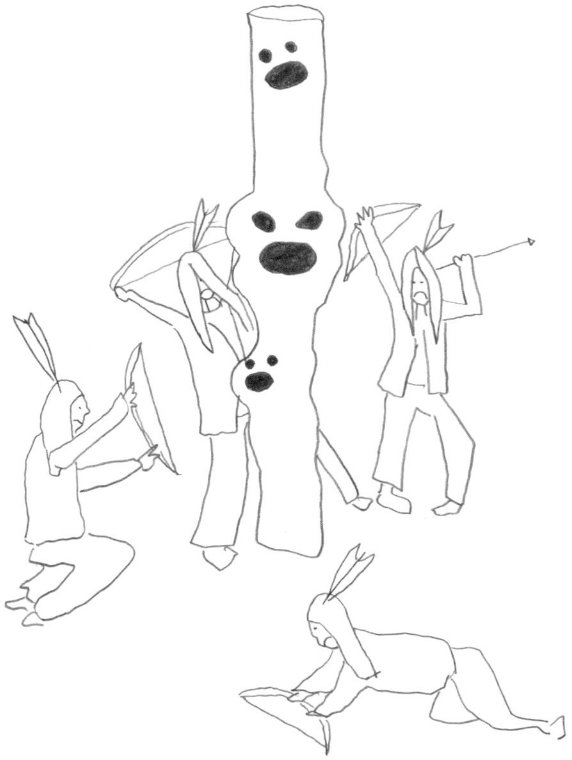

Indians
2005

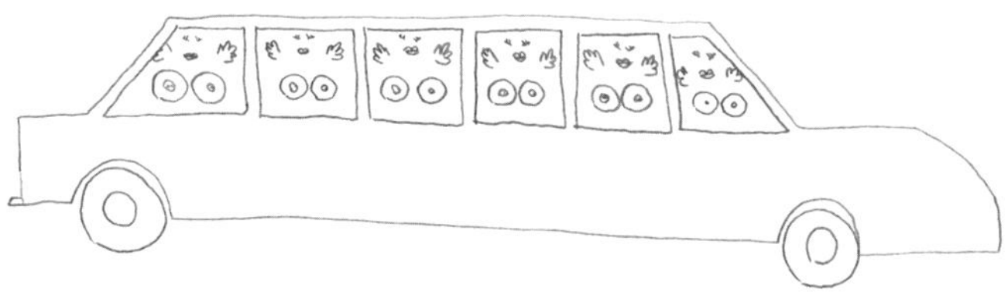

Boobilimi
2007

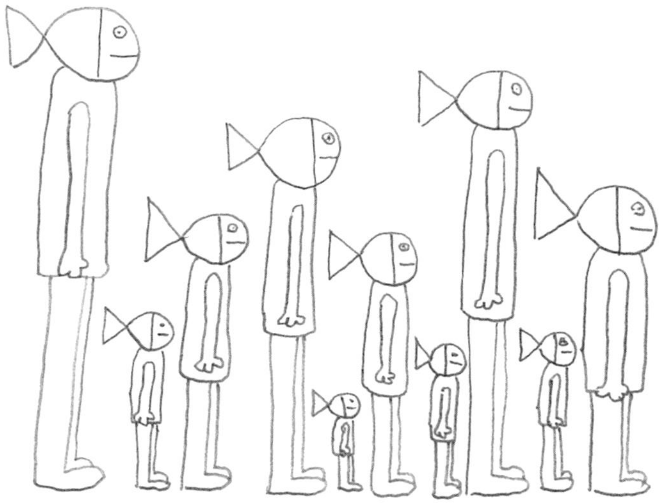

Fish or Woman
2007

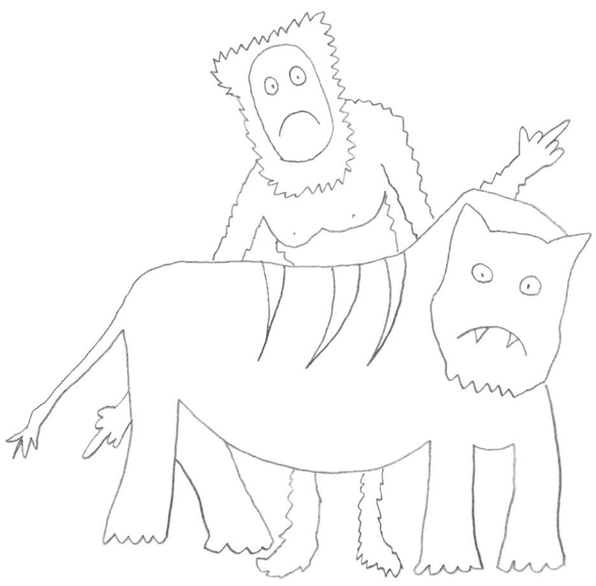

It Is Easy Behind a Tiger to Say Fuck You!
2005

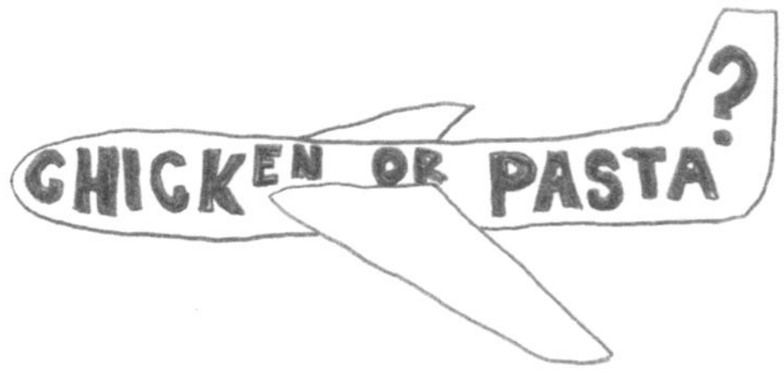

Chicken or Pasta?
2012

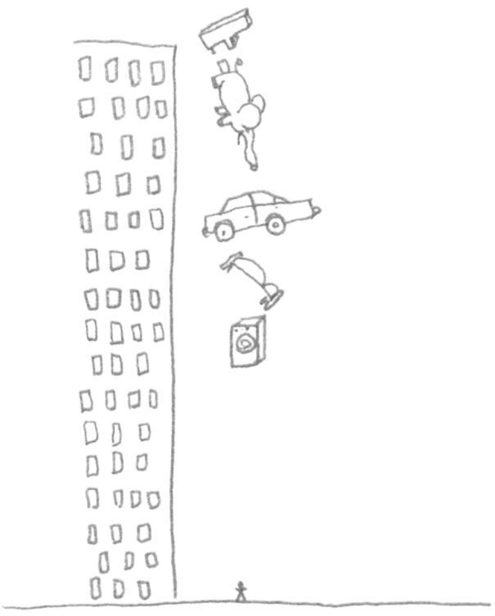

Just a Bad Day
2014

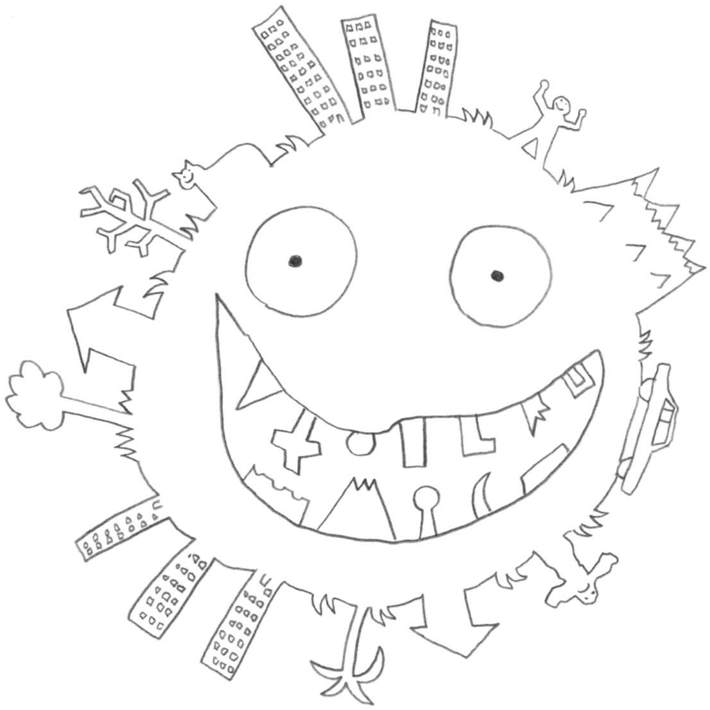

Don’t Trust the Earth
2005

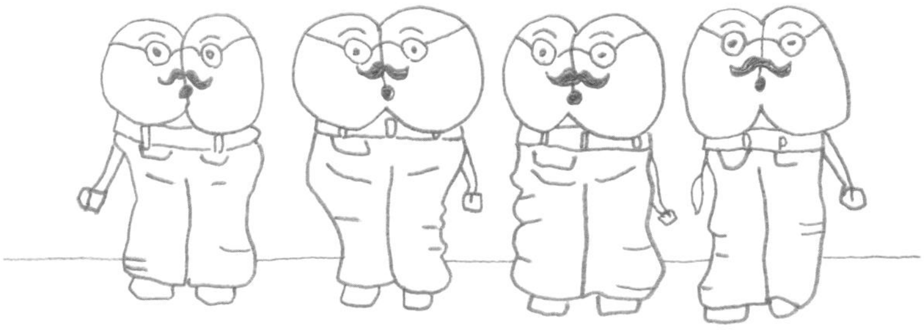

Assholes
2015

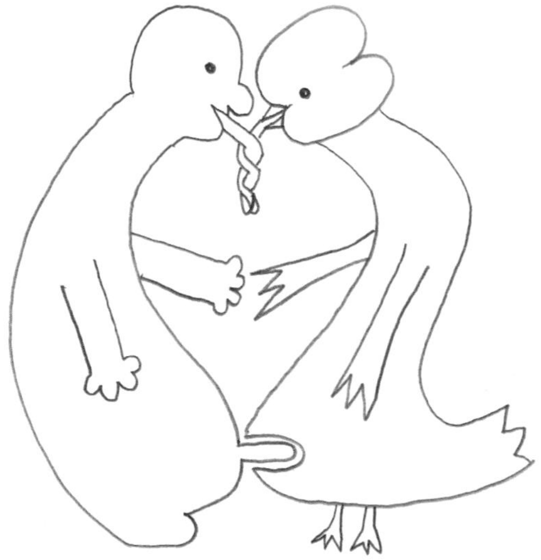

Hello Yves
2005

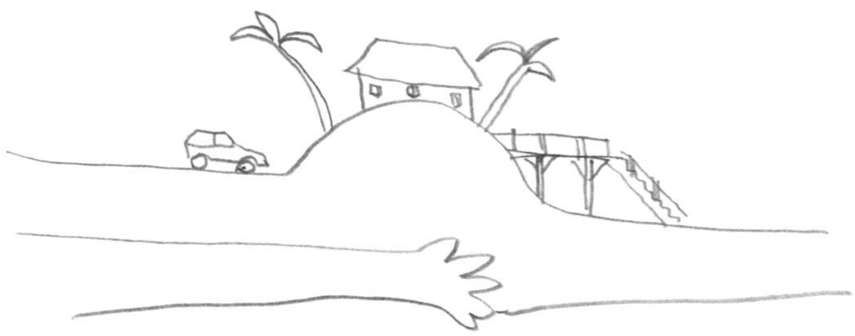

Dream House
2005

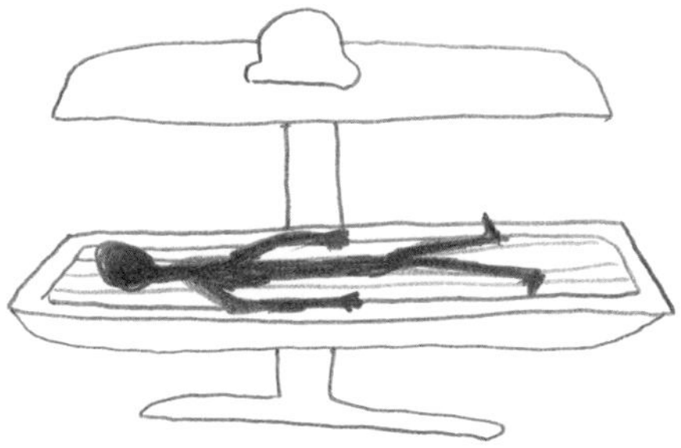

I Want to Be Bronze
2010

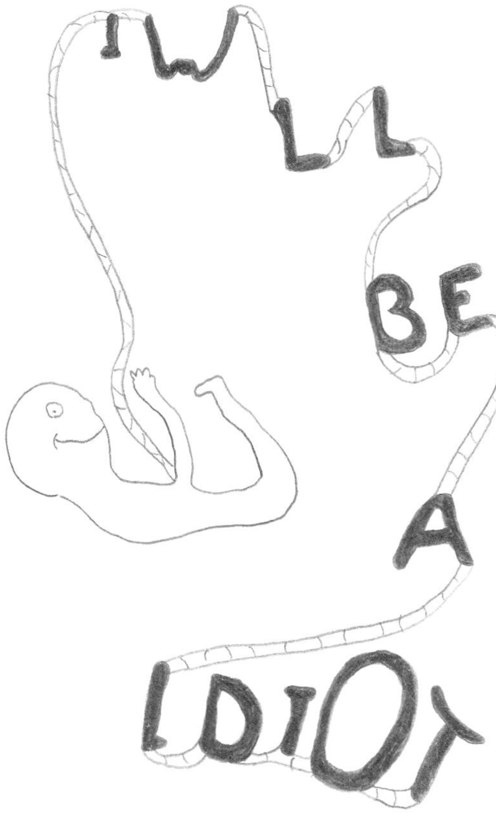

I Wll Be a Idiot
2005

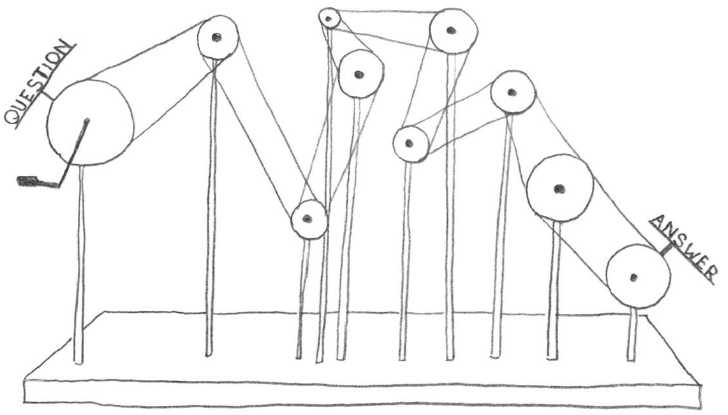

Question / Answer
2007

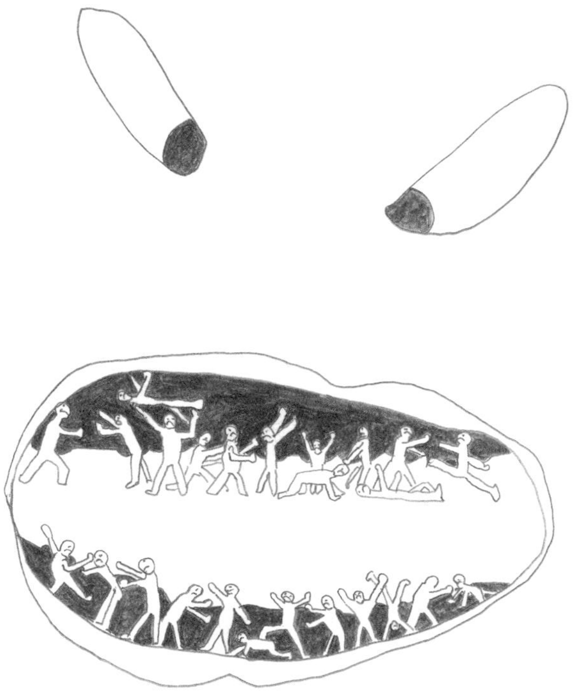

Angry Mouth
2005

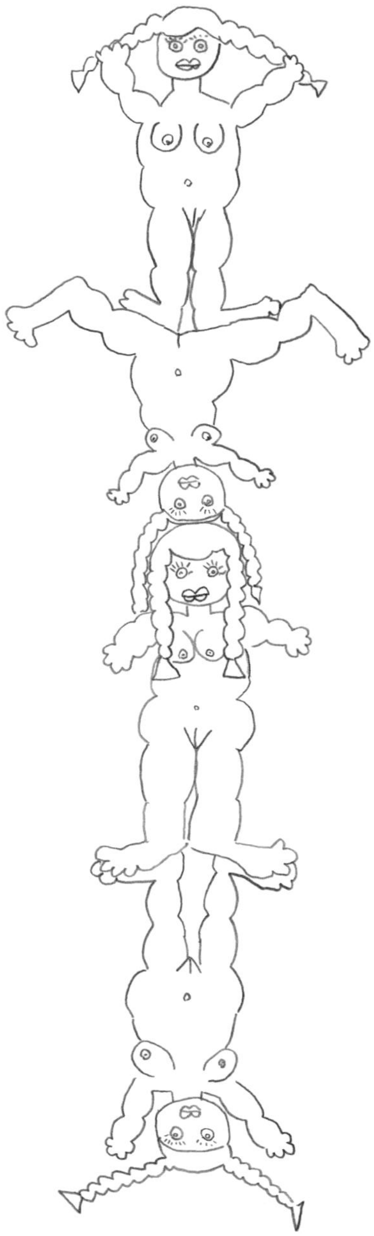

Bulgarian Dance Group
2005

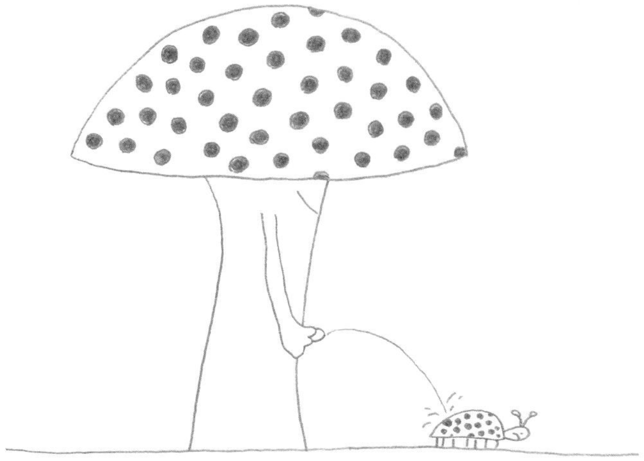

Bully
2015

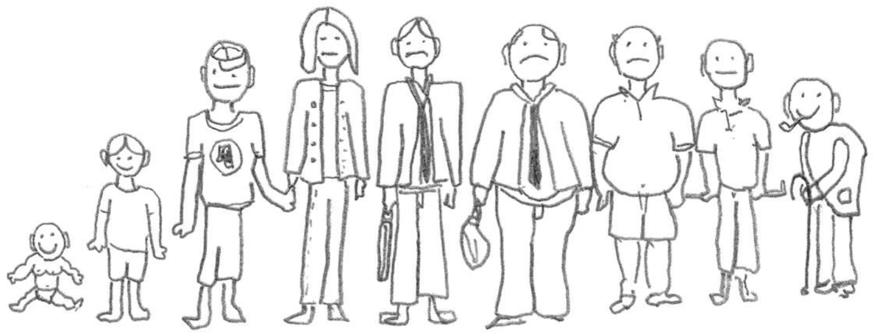

Don’t Worry the Smile Is Coming Back Later
2007

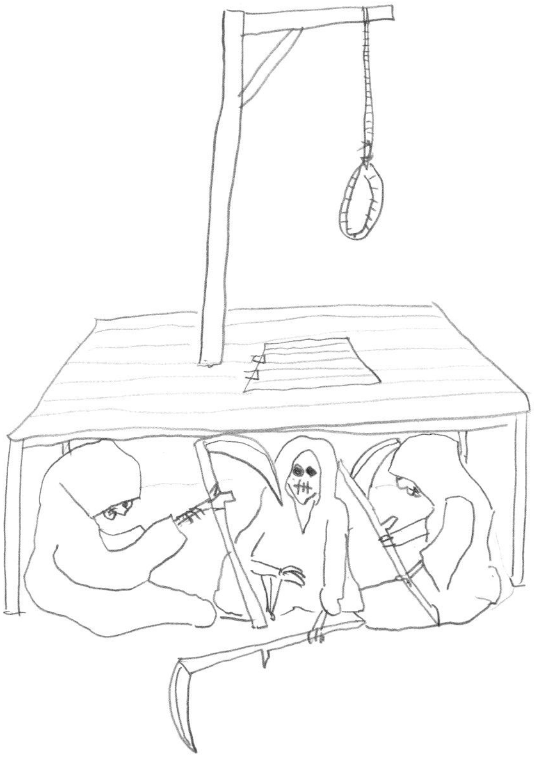

Death Has to Be Tired of Waiting
2005

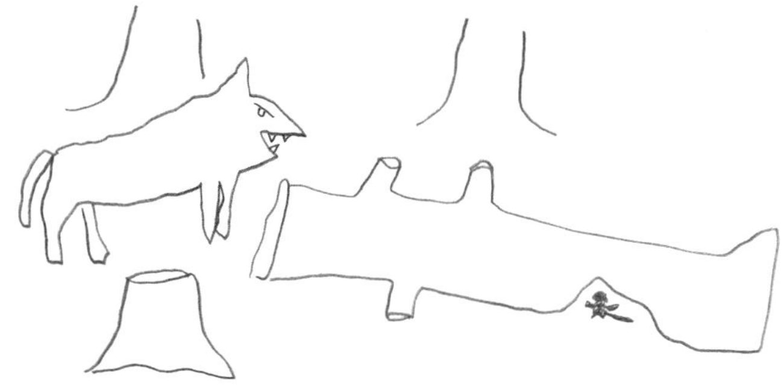

Bad Animal
2014

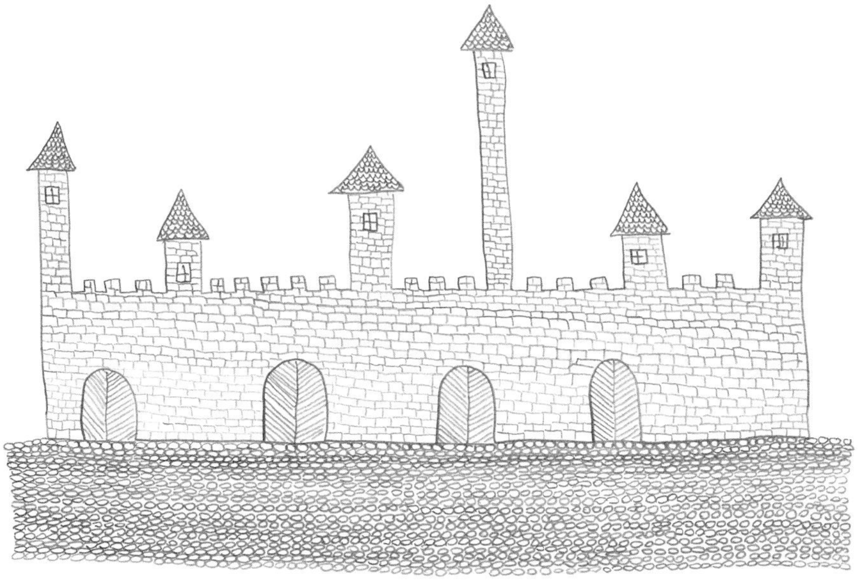

Castle
2005

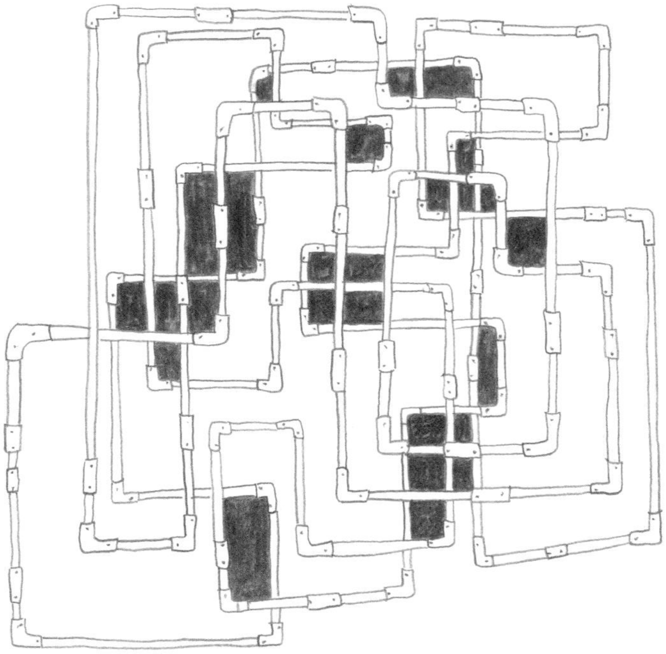

Art History
2005

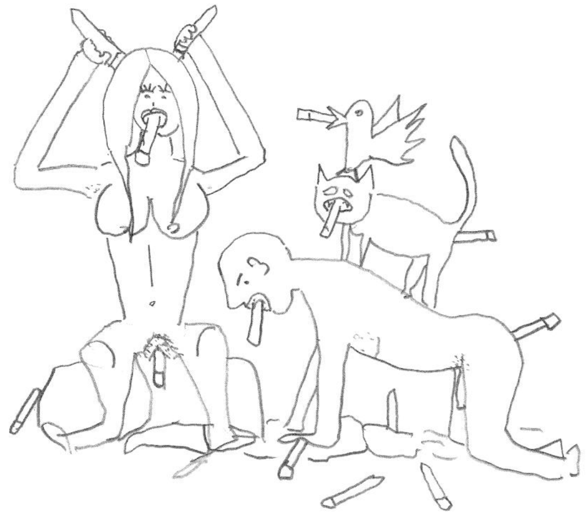

Lust
2005

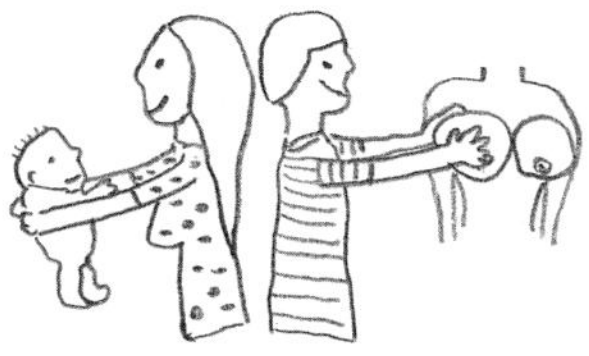

Force of Nature
2009

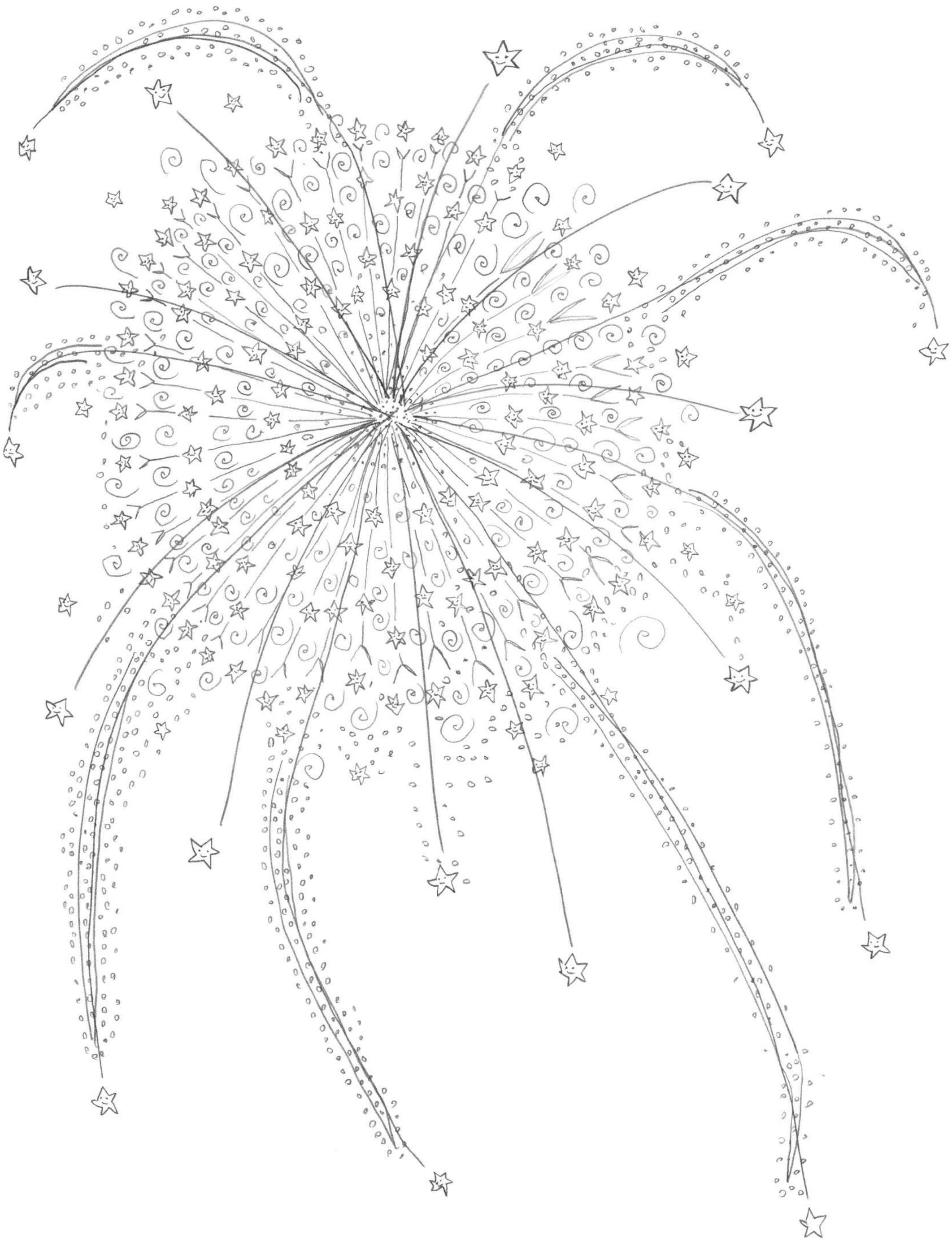

Firework
2005

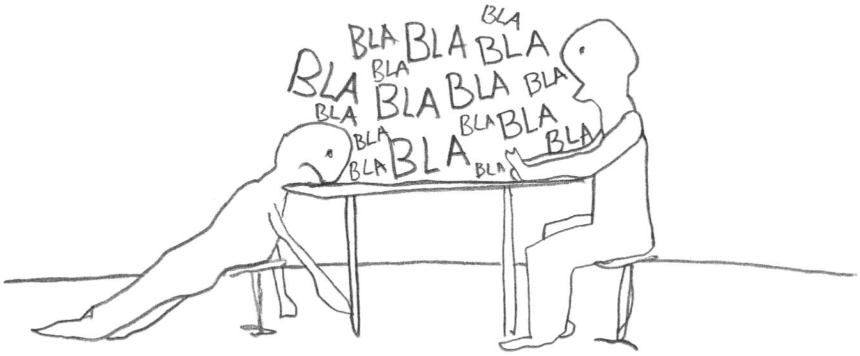

Bla Bla Bla
2007

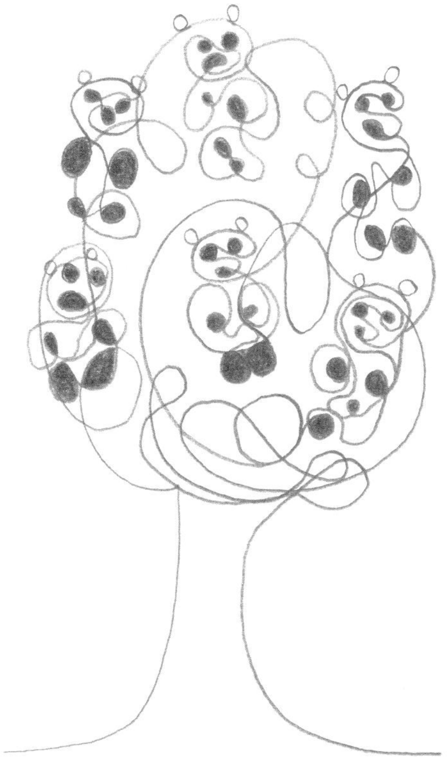

Pandas Hiding from the Predater
2015

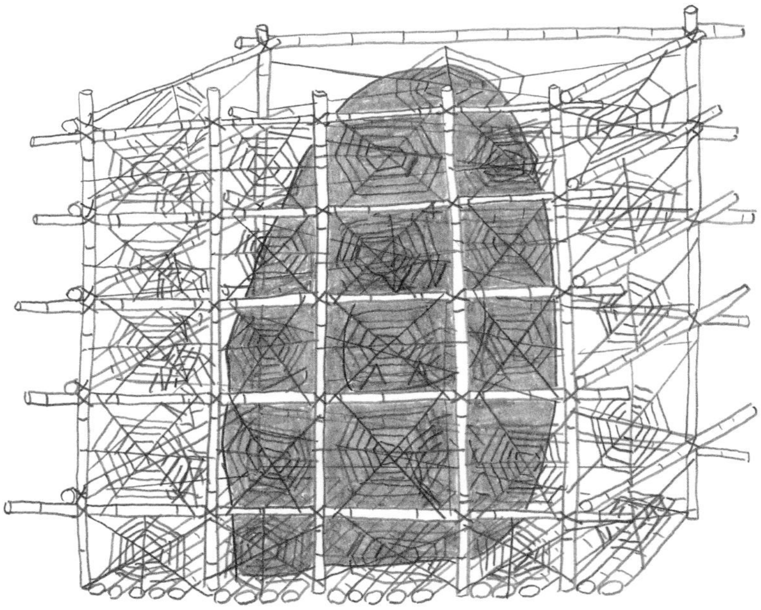

Gefangenes Ei
2005

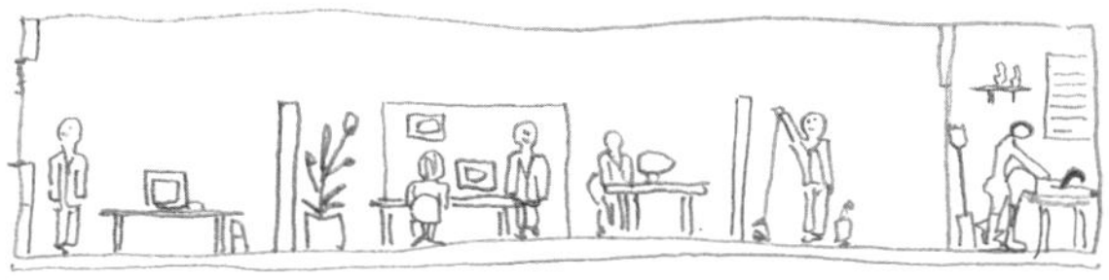

Quiet Afternoon in the Office
2012

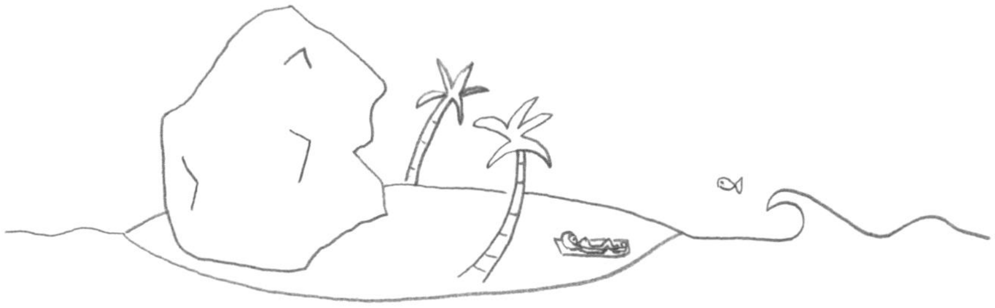

Fertile Nature
2013

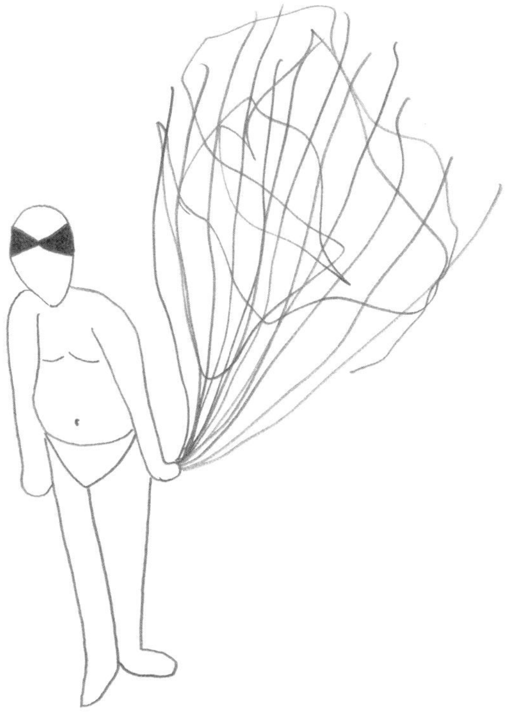

Brother of Spiderman
2005

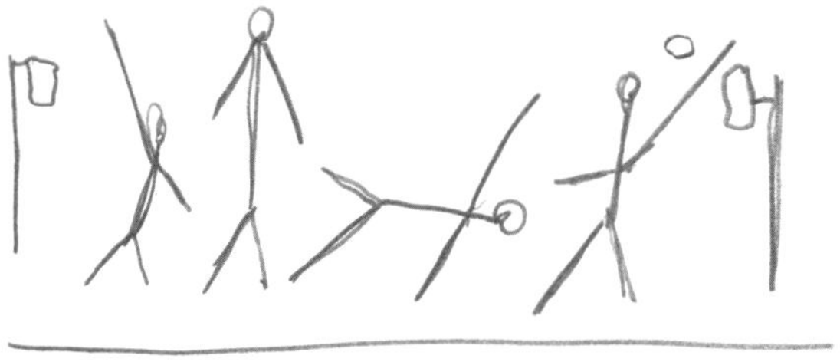

Basketball
2014

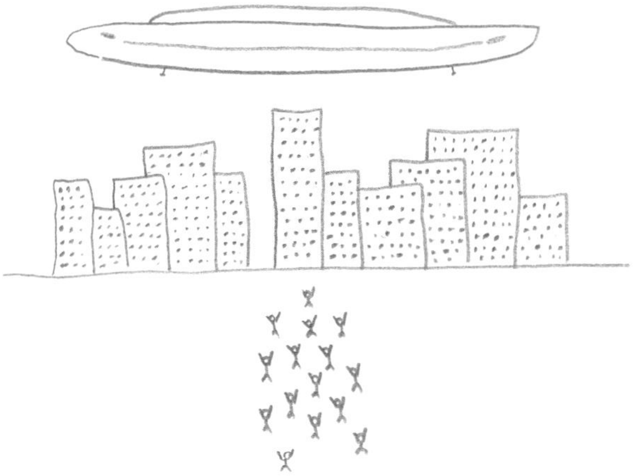

Invasion II
2016

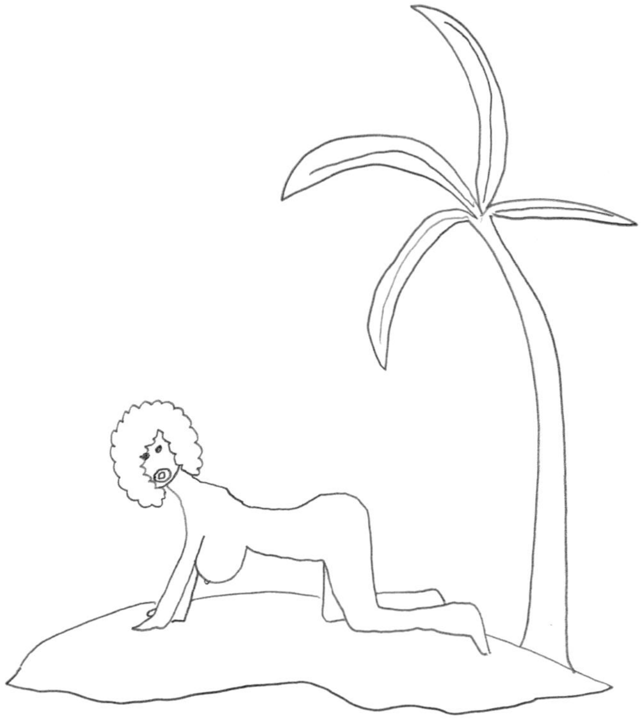

Dream Woman
2005

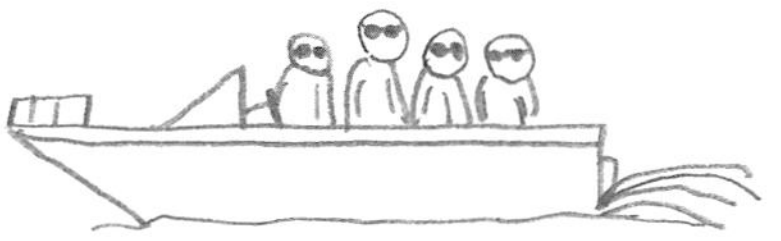

Cool Boat
2005

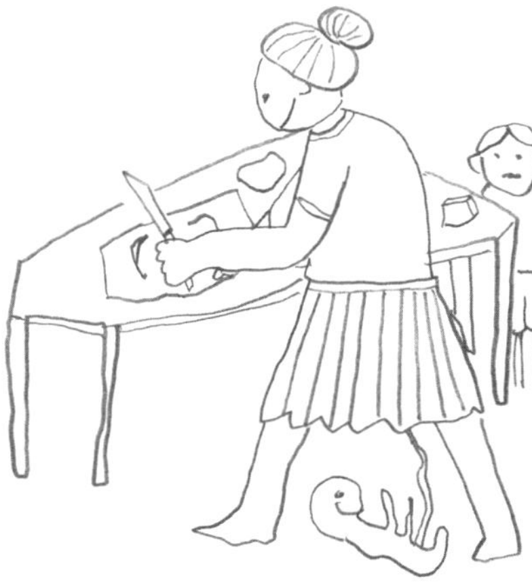

Mother Nature
2012

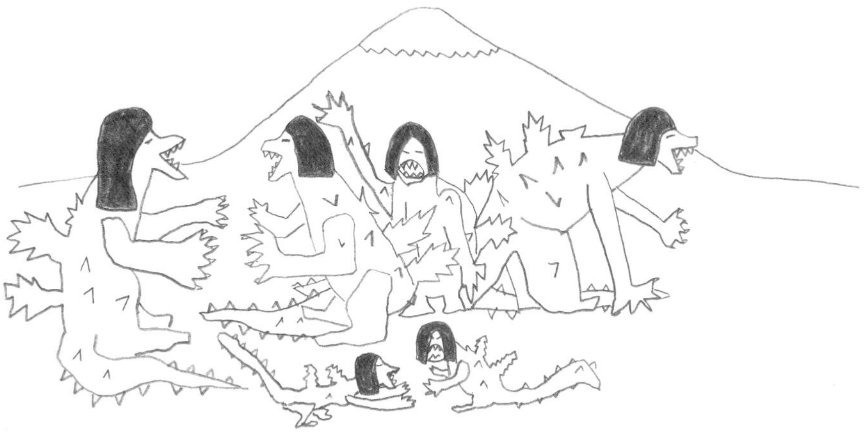

First Japanese
2010

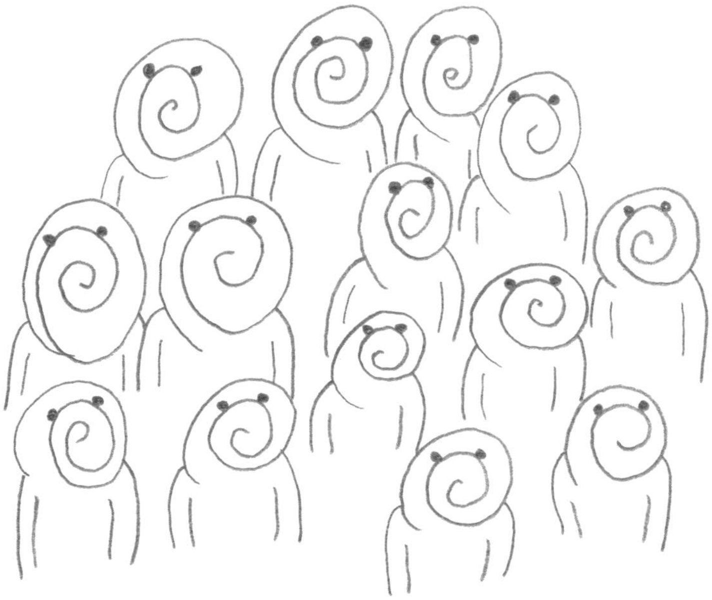

Mixerfaces
2015

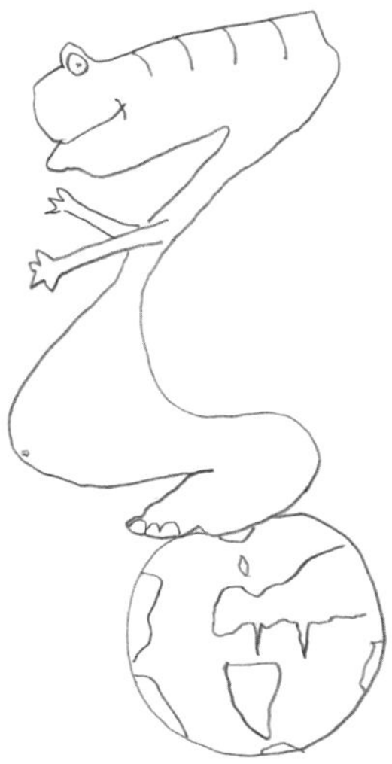

Is There Some Life Out There?
2005

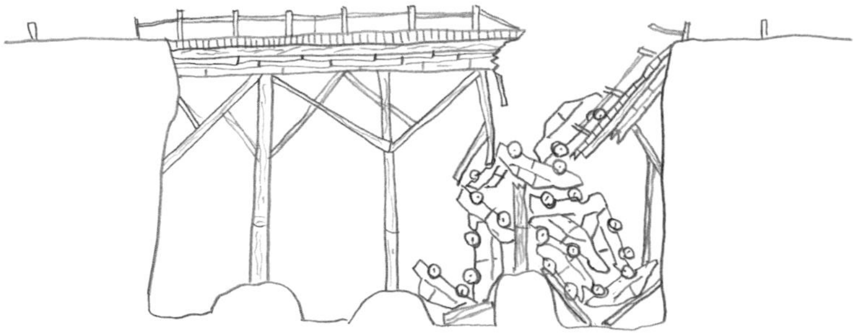

Too Many Cars
2005

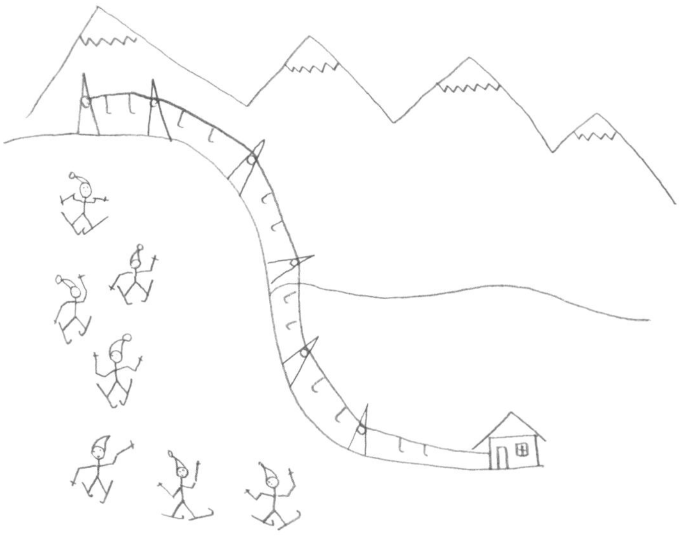

Swiss Mountains
2015

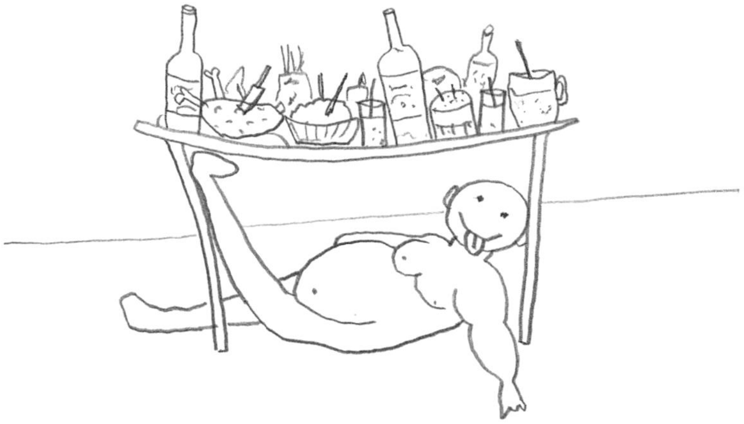

Good Life
2011

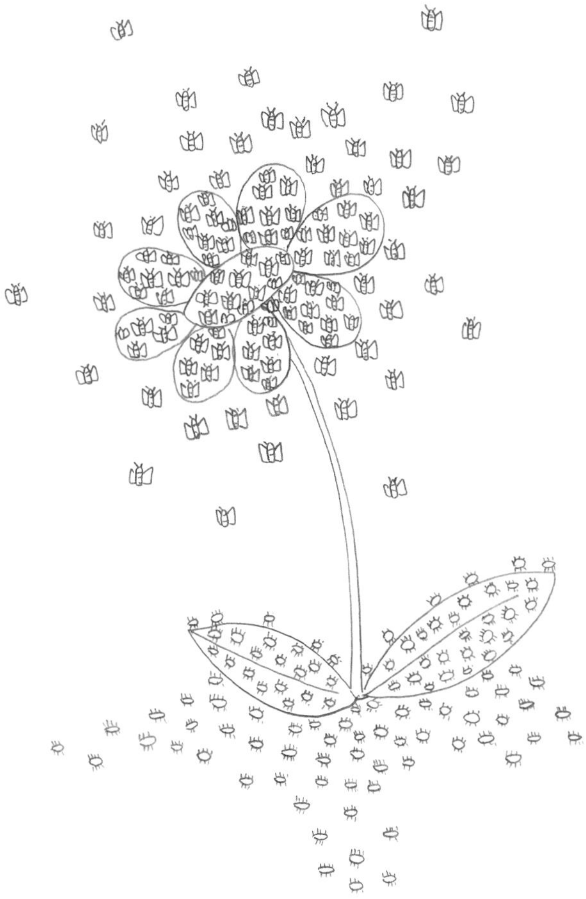

Bugs and Bees
2005

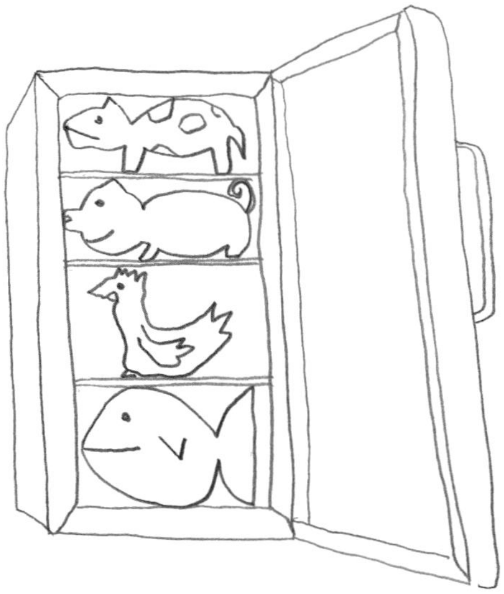

Cold Animals
2005

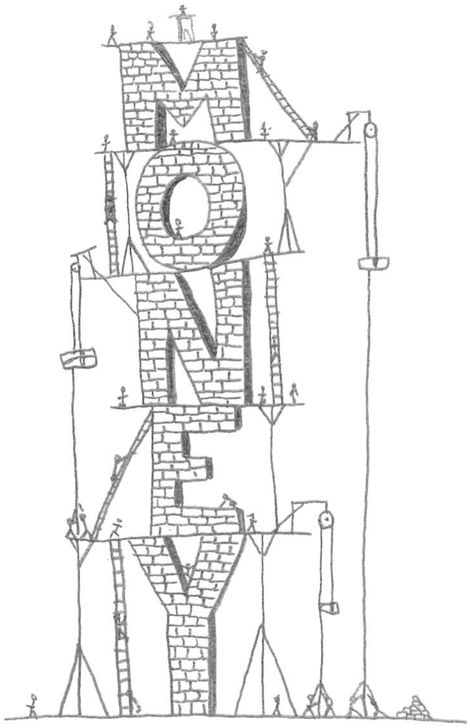

Always the Money
2012

Shooting
2013

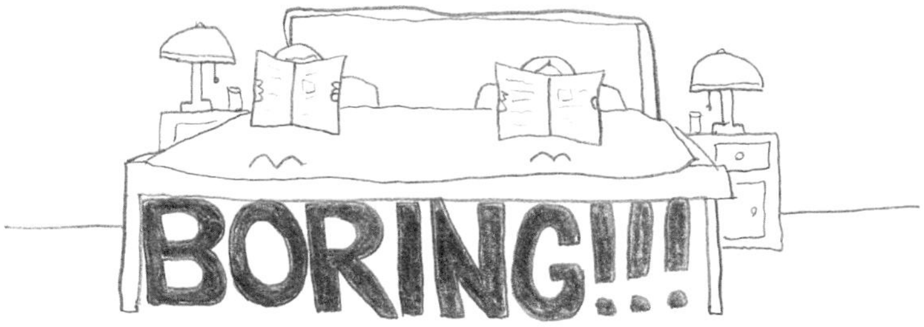

Boring but Nice
2012

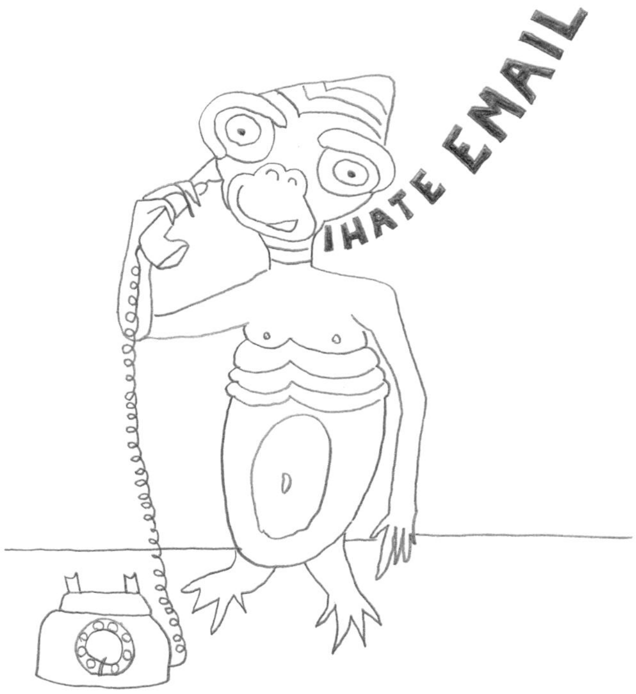

I Hate Email
2005

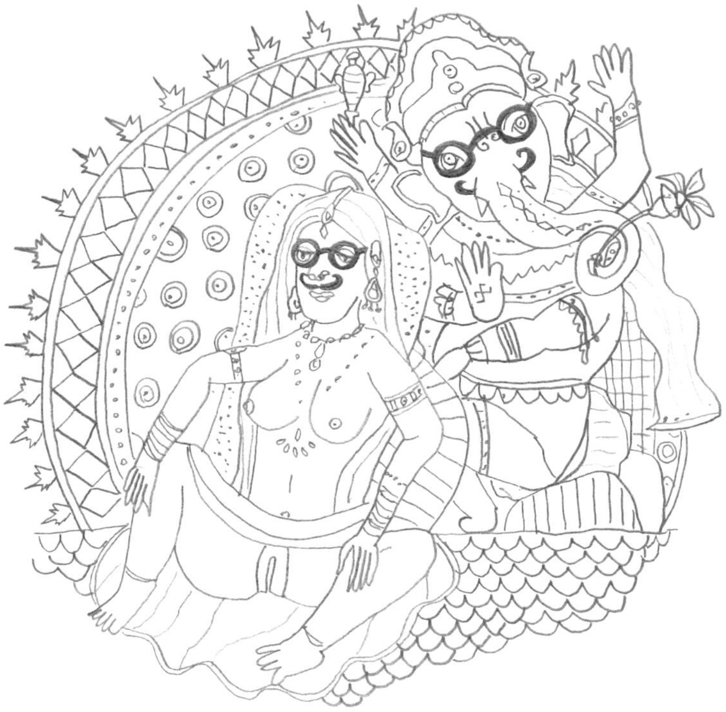

Glasses
2007

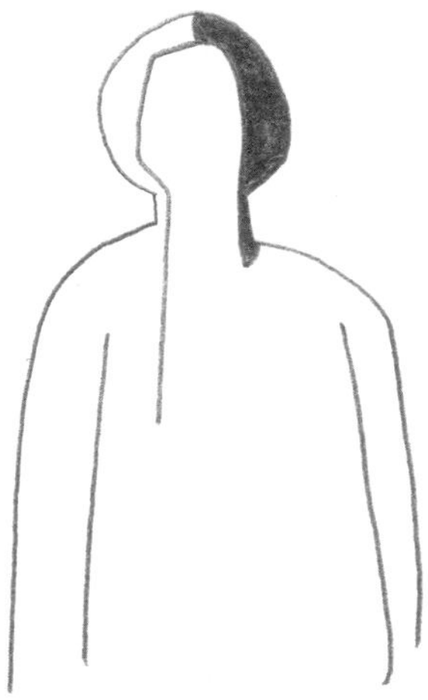

Split Personality
2015

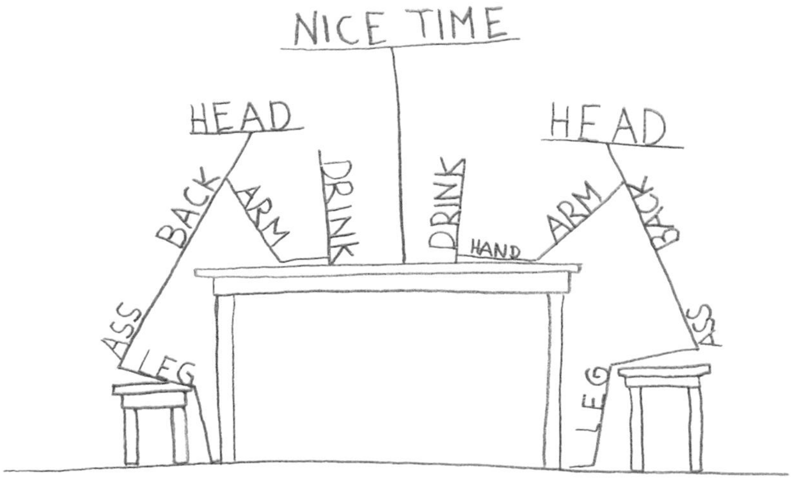

Nice Time
2011

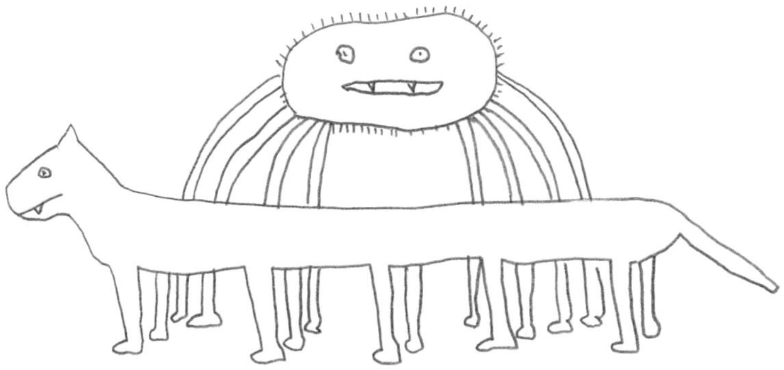

One Second, Whose Legs?
2005

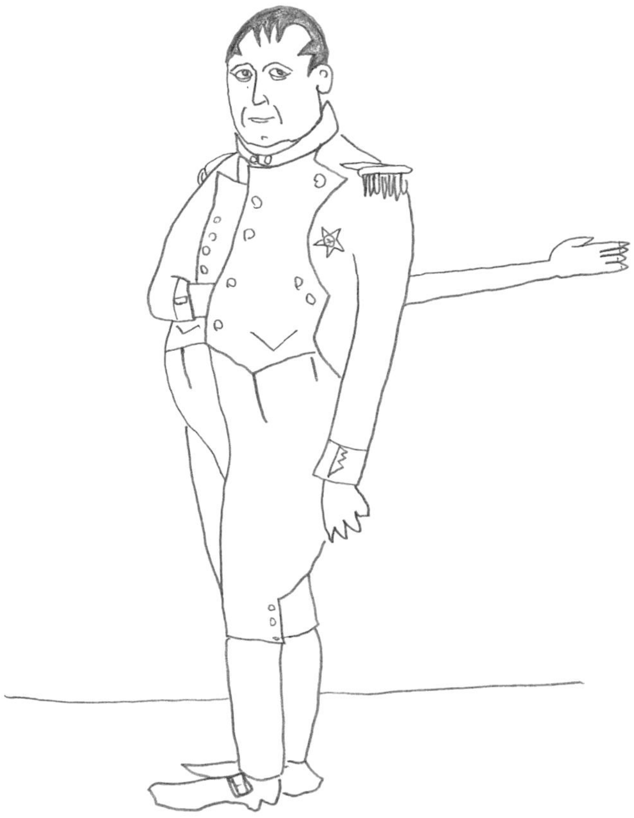

Napoleon
2008

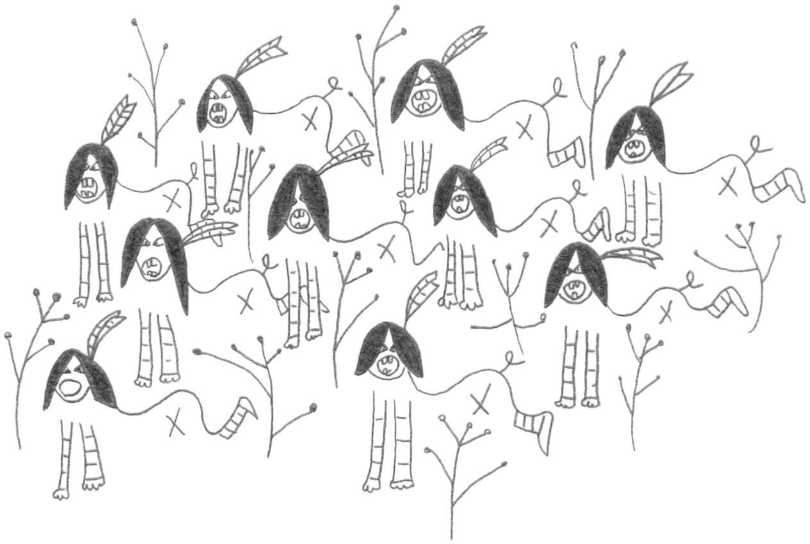

Indian Summer
2015

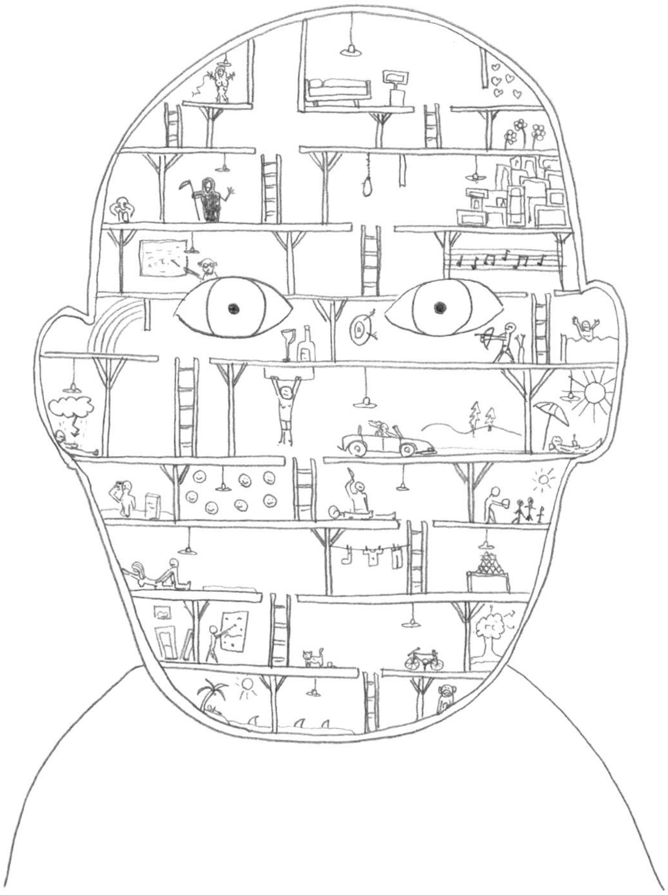

Too Many Things in My Head
2011

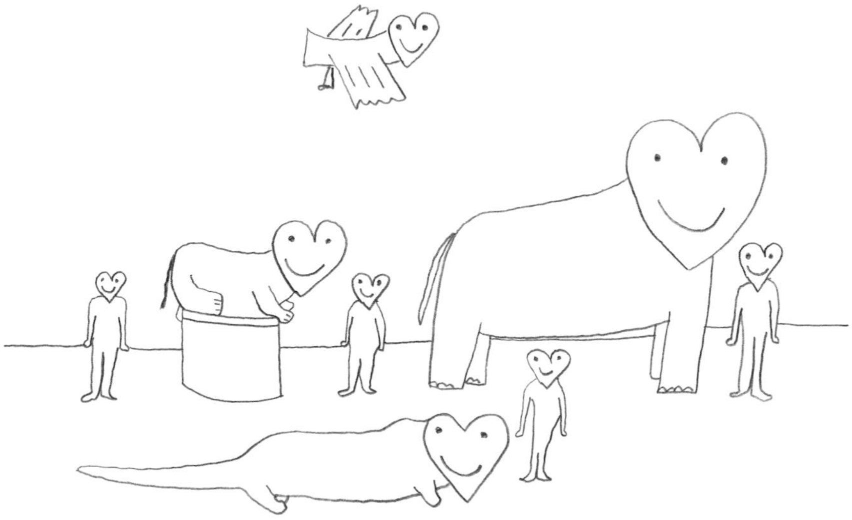

Peace Time
2013

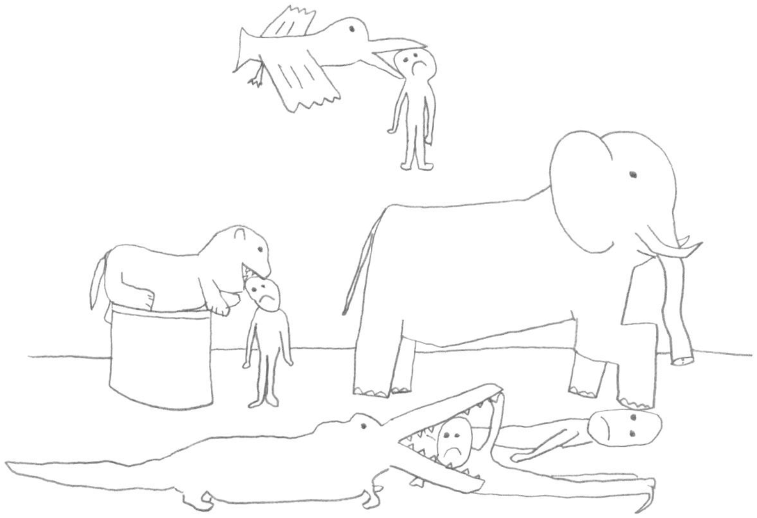

War Time
2013

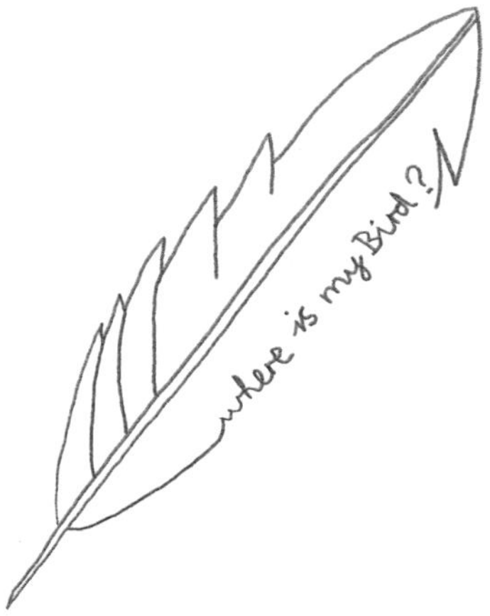

Where Is My Bird?
2014

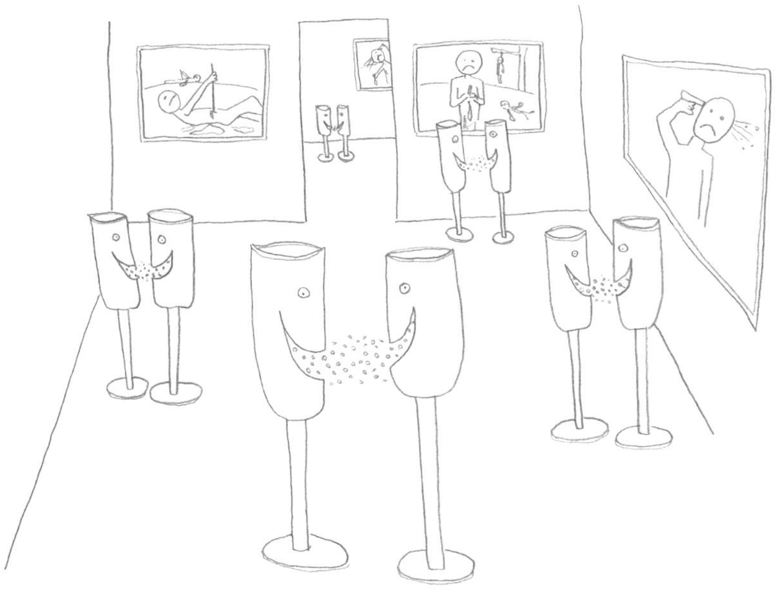

My Opening
2008

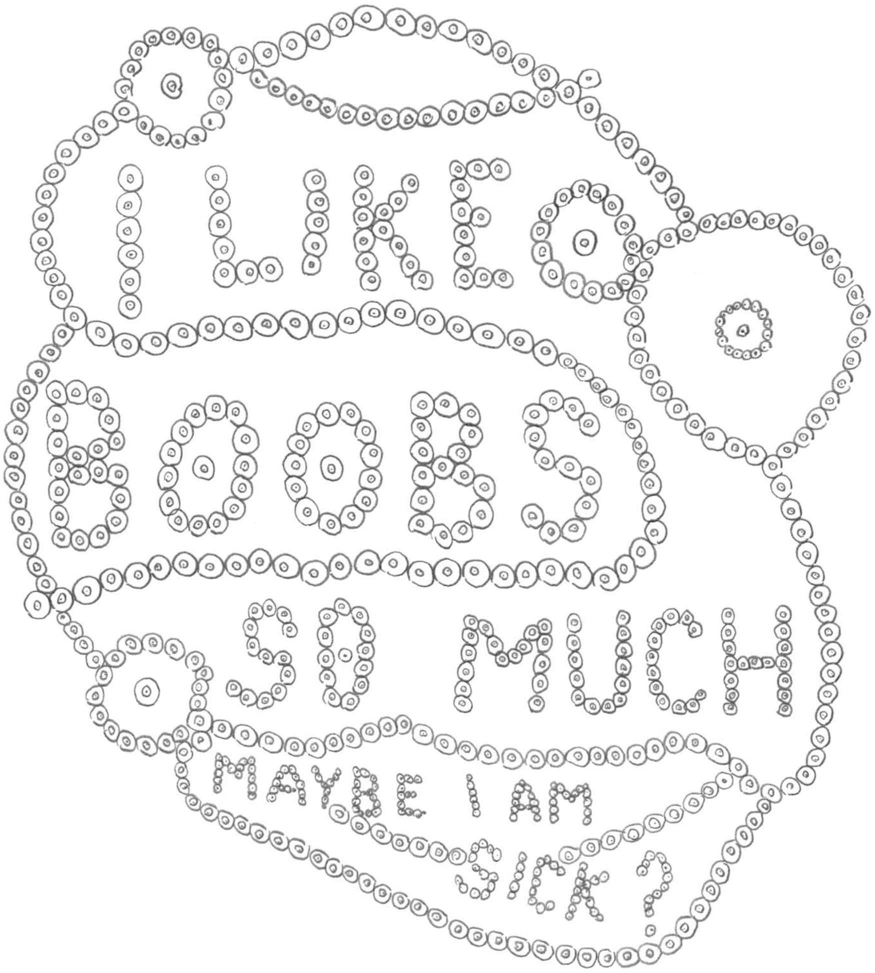

I Like Boobs
2008

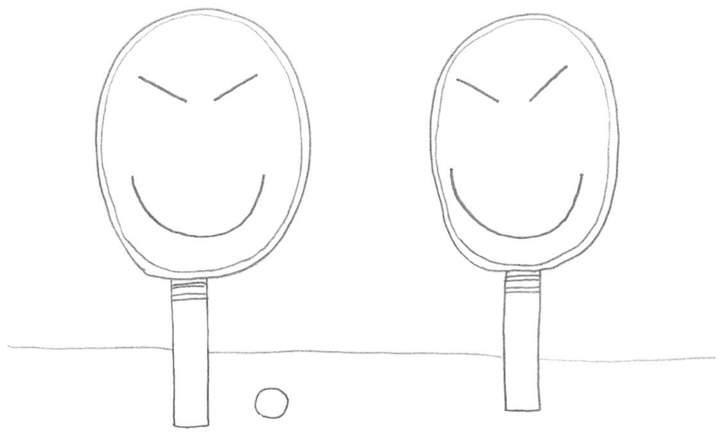

Mr. Ping and Mr. Pong
2011

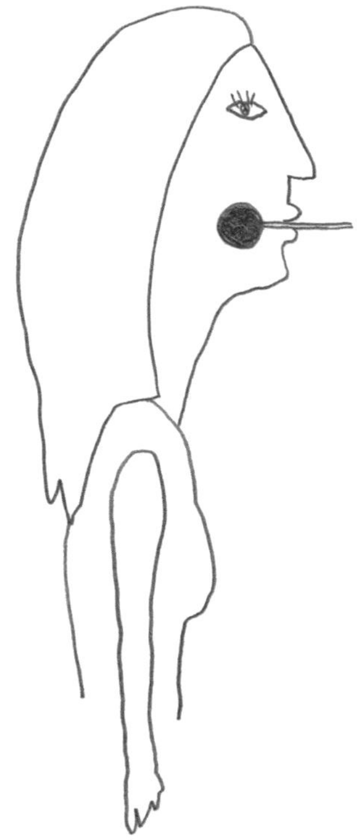

Lolli
2008

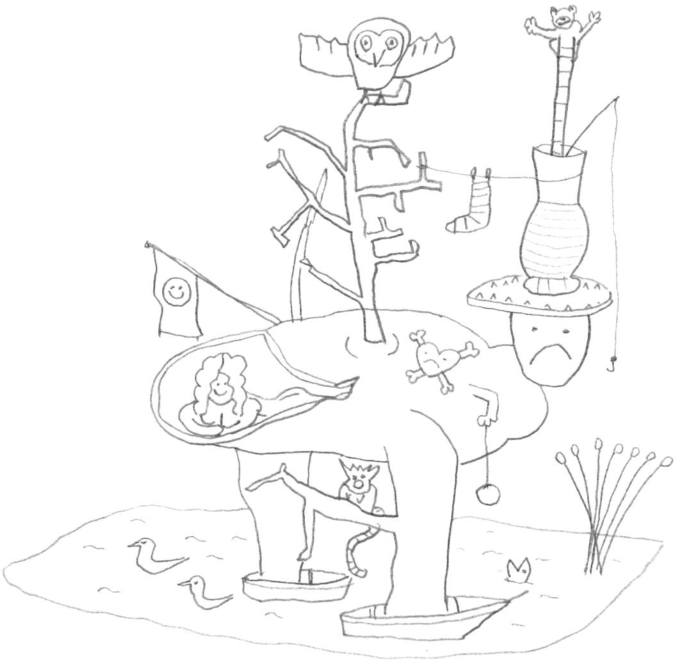

Hironimus Hosch
2008

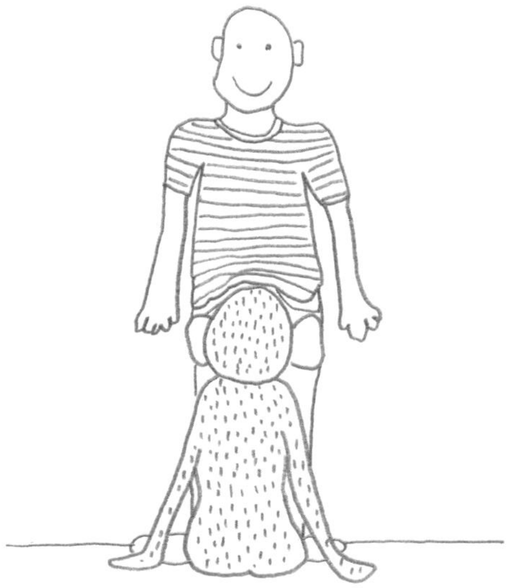

Blowjob Monkey
2012

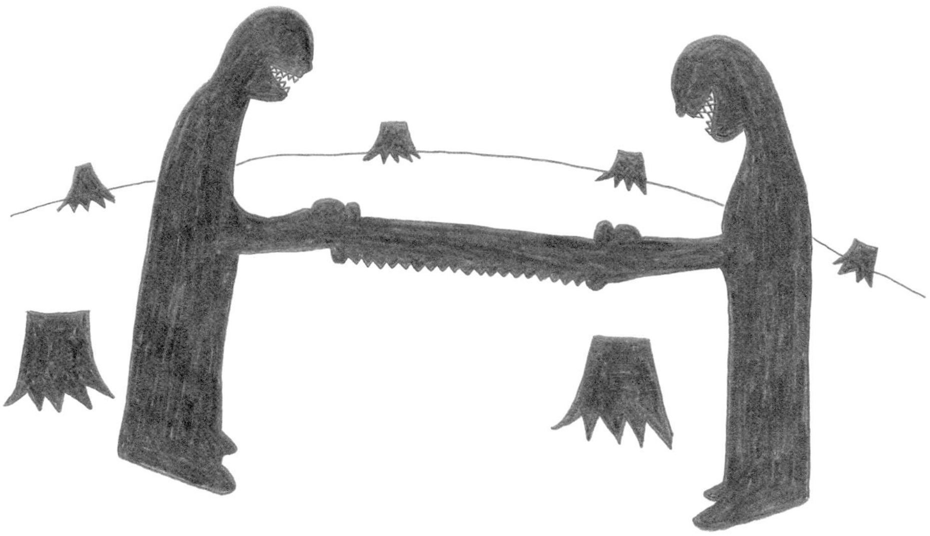

Saw Men
2009

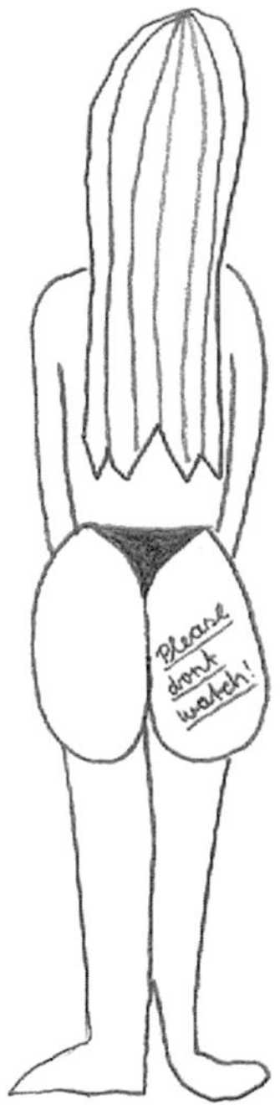

Please Don't Watch
2015

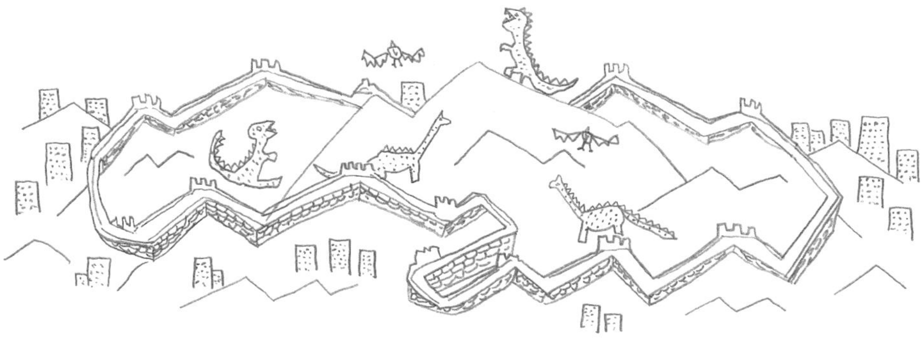

Keep the Dragons Behind the Wall
2008

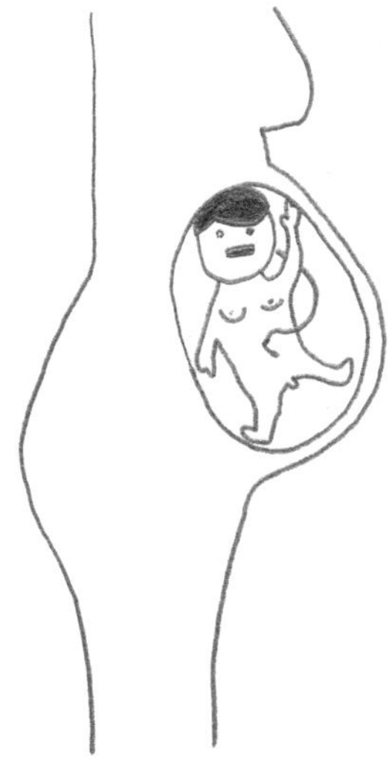

Small Adolf
2015

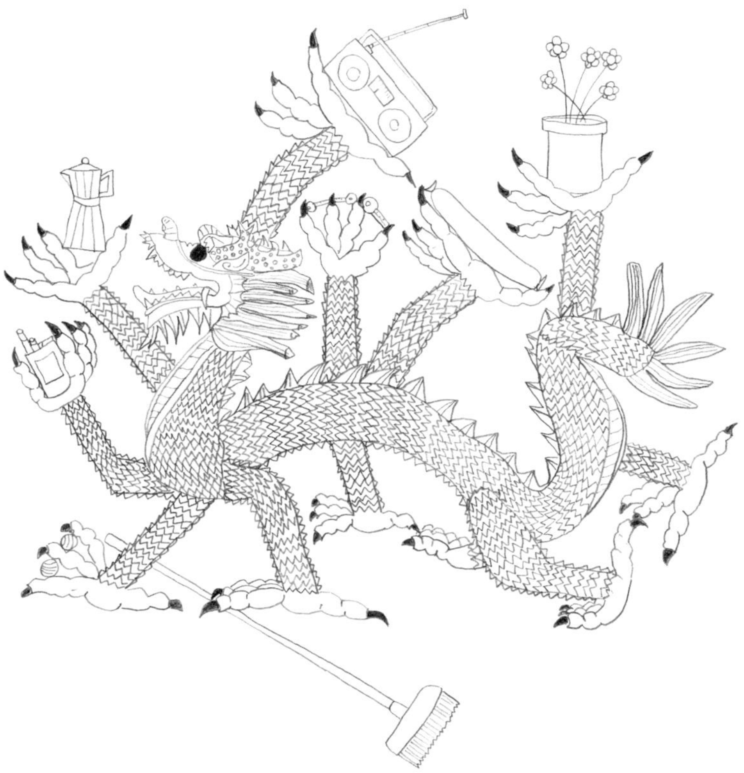

Comfort Dragon
2005

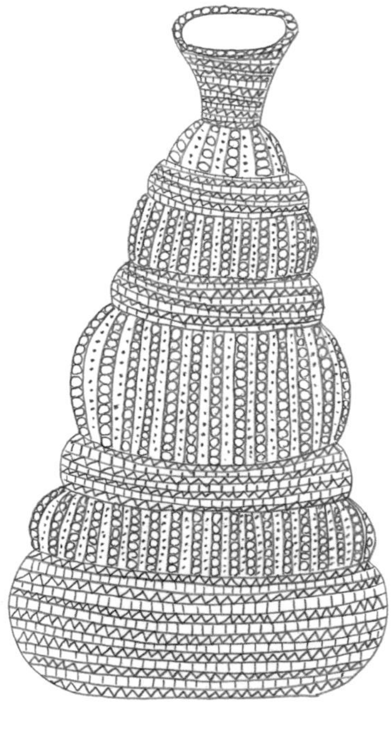

Vase
2005

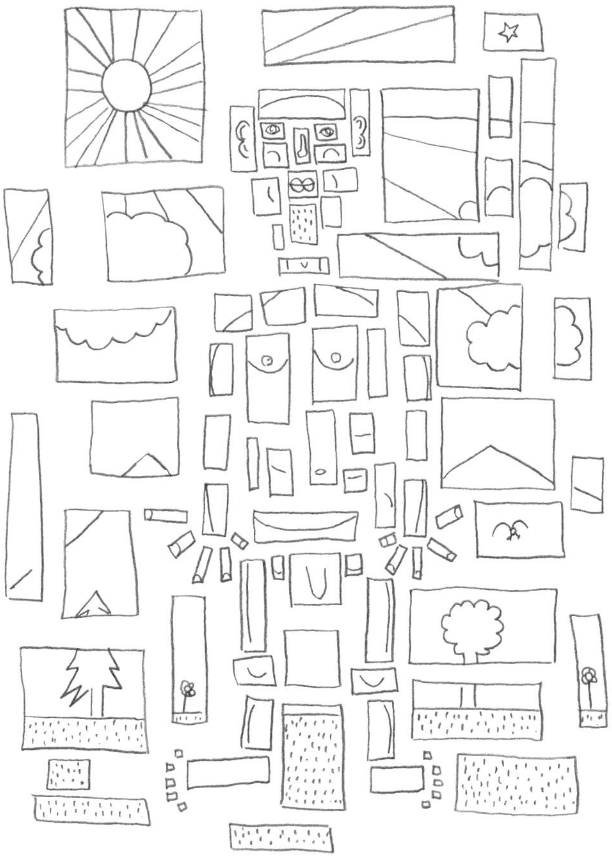

Can't Focus Anymore
2011

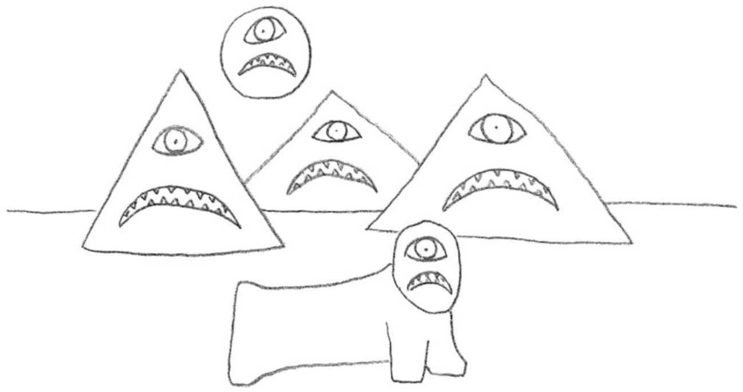

The Eyes
2015

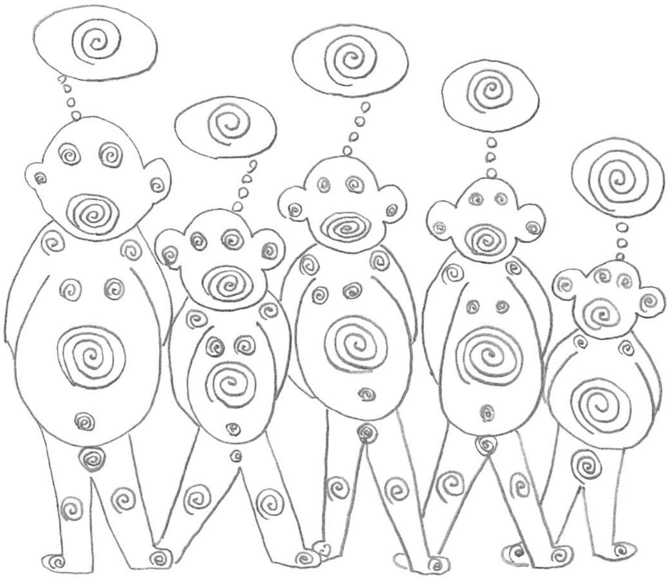

We Are What We Are
2009

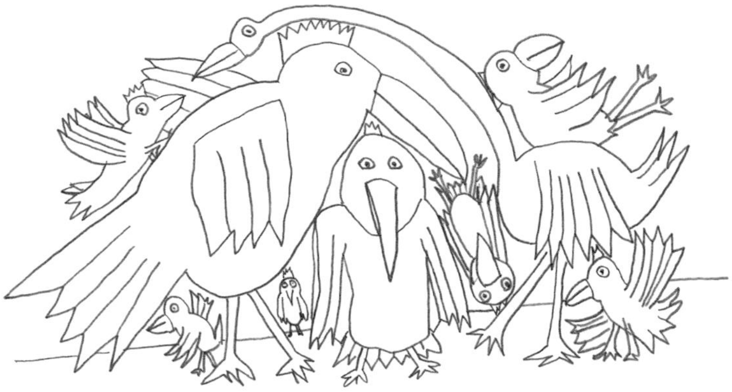

Vögel
2015

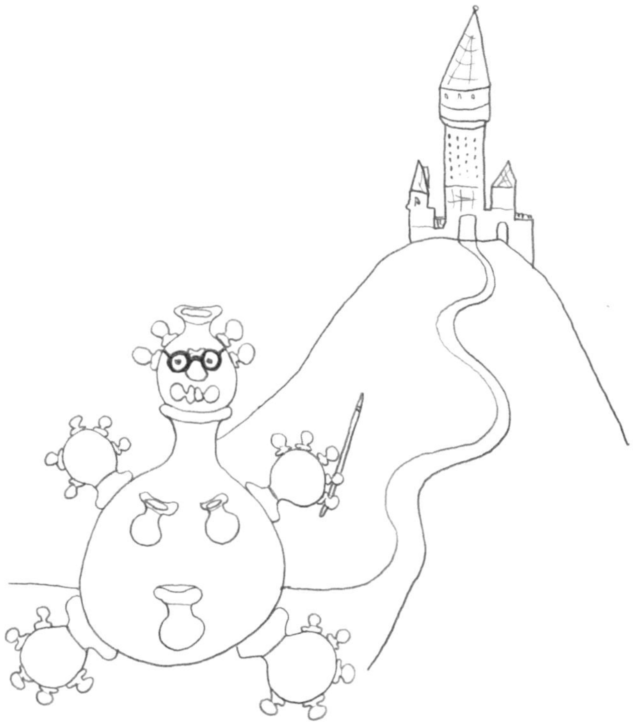

Harry Pottery
2010

Big thanks to my galleries who have supported me over the years and made this book happen:

Metro Pictures, New York
Nils Stærk, Copenhagen
Carbon12, Dubai
Galerie Nicola von Senger, Zurich
Michael Benevento, Los Angeles
Kodama Gallery, Tokyo

And a special thanks to:
Verlag für moderne Kunst, Silvia Jaklitsch, Makiko Aoki, Angelina Z. Knight, Elsy Lahner, Brett Littman, Emi Shiokawa, Restaurant Balthazar, my humor, Queen Mary II (not the real queen) and all the people involved in showing and liking my drawings.

Cover
Talk to the Hand
2010

All drawings in this book were made between 2005 and 2016, the originals are pencil on paper, 8.5 × 11 inch (21.6 × 27.9 cm). Some of them have or might become large scale ink and wall drawings, or sculptures made of different materials.

This drawing book complements the monograph designed by Dominique Clausen, published by Gestalten, Berlin 2016.

Brett Littman has been the Executive Director of The Drawing Center since 2007. Previously he was the Deputy Director of MoMA PS1, Co-Director of Dieu Donné papermill and Associate Director of UrbanGlass. He has contributed news and commentary to a wide range of international publications and critical essays to many exhibition catalogues. As a curator, Littman has organized exhibitions for The Drawing Center and other non-profits and galleries worldwide.

Elsy Lahner is among Austria's leading experts on contemporary drawing and young Austrian art. In 2007, she co-founded and managed one of Austria's most lively independent art spaces "das weisse haus" (the white house), realizing various exhibition projects in a number of different vacant buildings all over Vienna. Elsy was curator-in-residence at the Academy of Fine Arts in Vienna in 2008/2009 and initiated a foundation for art and knowledge transfer in Yokohama and Vienna. Since 2011, she is curator for contemporary art at the Albertina.

Published by:
Verlag für moderne Kunst
Editor: Olaf Breuning
Graphic Design: Angelina Z. Knight

Authors: Elsy Lahner, Brett Littman

Translation:
Alexandra Cox (Elsy Lahner)
Proofreading:
Michaela Alex-Eibensteiner

Printing: Holzhausen Druck GmbH, Wolkersdorf, Austria

VfmK Verlag für moderne Kunst GmbH
Salmgasse 4a
1030 Vienna
Austria
hello@vfmk.org
www.vfmk.org

ISBN 978-3-903131-47-7

Distribution
Germany, Austria, and other European Countries: LKG, www.lkg-va.de
Switzerland: AVA, www.ava.ch
UK: Cornerhouse Publications, www.cornerhousepublications.org
USA: D.A.P., www.artbook.com

Bibliographic information published by Die Deutsche Nationalbibliothek
Die Deutsche Nationalbibliothek lists this publication in the Deutsche Nationalbibliografie; detailed bibliographic data is available on the Internet at http://dnb.ddb.de